ROCK MUSIC! DEATH!
CRAZY PEOPLE! LOVE!

Growing up in the Virginia suburbs, Mark Oliver Everett had an *Ice Storm*–like existence, left to roam unsupervised with his sister, Liz, while his mother combated depression and his father, the eccentric and brilliant quantum physicist Hugh Everett, remained distant and obsessed by parallel universes of his own creation. First, the author lost his father to heart failure, and then—in a staggeringly short period of time—his sister to schizophrenia and suicide and his mother to cancer. The author drew upon the relentless tragedies in his life for inspiration in writing highly acclaimed music with his indie rock group, the Eels. Yet this is much more than a musician's tale. A true gem of a memoir, Everett's story is a rich and poignant narrative on coming of age, love, death, and the creative vision.

"[Everett is] the Kurt Vonnegut of the rock world."

—*Rolling Stone*

"I kept telling myself, 'This guy is the next Kurt Vonnegut!' *Things the Grandchildren Should Know* shares less with a rock memoir than it does with the likes of *The Corrections, Middlesex*, and *The Ice Storm*. It's unexpectedly uplifting."

—*The Word* (UK)

"His unique sensibility is as apparent in his prose as in his music. Even those unfamiliar with, or indifferent to, Everett's work will still vicariously enjoy meeting him."

—*The Independent* (UK)

"I learned more about my own business and my own methods by reading this book than I did by reading the life of Chuck Berry, Elvis, or David Bowie." —Pete Townshend

THINGS THE GRANDCHILDREN SHOULD KNOW

MARK OLIVER EVERETT

THOMAS DUNNE BOOKS
ST. MARTIN'S PRESS ≈ NEW YORK

THOMAS DUNNE BOOKS.
An imprint of St. Martin's Press.

THINGS THE GRANDCHILDREN SHOULD KNOW. Copyright © 2008 by Mark Oliver Everett. All rights reserved. Printed in the United States of America. For information, address St. Martin's Press, 175 Fifth Avenue, New York, N.Y. 10010.

www.thomasdunnebooks.com
www.stmartins.com

"This Was the Vision" from *Music of the Morning,* copyright 1937, Katharine Kennedy, The Banner Press, Atlanta

All EELS lyrics © Mark Oliver Everett

"Happy Trails" from the Television series *The Roy Rogers Show*. Words and Music by Dale Evans. Copyright © 1951, 1952 (Renewed 1979, 1980) by Paramount—Roy Rogers Music Company, Inc. All rights administered by Sony/ATV Music Publishing LLC. 8 Music Square West, Nashville, TN 37203. All rights reserved. Used by permission.

"Rednecks" Words and music by Randy Newman © 1974, 1975 (Copyright renewed) WB Music Corp. All rights reserved. Used by Permission of Alfred Publishing Co., Inc.

                   Library of Congress Cataloging-in-Publication Data
Everett, Mark.
     Things the grandchildren should know / Mark Oliver Everett.—
1st U.S. ed.
           p. cm.
     Originally published: Great Britain : Little, Brown, 2008
     ISBN-13: 978-0-312-38513-2
     ISBN-10: 0-312-38513-7
     1. Everett, Mark. 2. Rock musicians—United States—Biography.
I. Title.

ML420.E96A3 2008
781.66092—dc22
[B]

                                                   2008024994

First Edition: September 2008

First published in Great Britain by Little, Brown

10 9 8 7 6 5 4 3 2 1

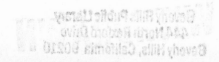

For Liz,
Hugh and Nancy,
wherever you are

CONTENTS

The following is a true story. Some names and hair colors have been changed.

1

SUMMER OF LOVE

I WAS DRIVING THROUGH THE PITCH BLACK VIR-
ginia night, down the perfectly flat blacktop that was once
a railroad track, across that high bridge over the ravine,
thinking about the details of how one night I was going to
drive off it. I was sure I'd never live to the age of eighteen,
so I never bothered making any plans for the future. Eighteen had come and gone a year ago, but I was still breathing. And things were only getting worse.

The summer of 1982. That disgusting, sticky, humid
weather where your back soaks through your shirt just
from taking a short drive. By midsummer everything was
a mess. My sister Liz's boyfriend flipped out in our kitchen

one night and attacked me with a butcher knife. Soon after, Liz tried to kill herself for the first of many times. Swallowed a bunch of pills. Her heart stopped the moment we got her to the hospital, but they were able to revive her.

Pretty soon after that, Liz and my mom went out of town to visit relatives and I found my father's dead body lying there sideways on my parents' bed, fully dressed in his usual shirt and tie, with his feet almost on the floor, like he just sat down to die at fifty-one. I tried to learn CPR from the 911 operator on the phone, carrying my father's already-stiff body across the bedroom floor. It was weird touching him. That was the first time we had any physical contact that I could remember, other than the occasional cigarette burn on my arm while squeezing by him in the hallway.

I figured driving off the bridge might be the best way to deal with the crushing, lost, and empty feeling of being me. A dramatic way to go, of course. I was a kid. Later in life it would usually be a gun I imagined using on myself. Not quite as dramatic as driving off a bridge in your hometown. You can chart my development this way. In more recent years I would think about pills most often. That dramatic stuff is for kids. I'm mature now.

At the end of the summer, which I had already started referring to as The Summer of Love, I drove my gold '71 Chevy Nova away from home for the first time. I had bought the car that I called "Old Gold," complete with a stop sign used in place of its rusted-out floorboard, for a hundred bucks from my hot, blonde cousin Jennifer, who years later would die on the plane that hit the Pentagon September 11, 2001. She was a flight attendant. Sent a postcard from Dulles Airport that morning that read "Ain't Life Grand?" in big letters on the front.

My father worked at the Pentagon back around the time I was born. If I believed in curses, I'd have to wonder if the plane hit the part of the building where my father's office once was. But I don't believe in curses. Life is full of ups and downs. There have been some extremes in my life's case but, considering I had no plan, and very little of the kind of self-esteem you need to get by in this world, things could be worse. I'm just wandering through here, seeing what happens.

I don't know what happens when you die and I don't expect to find out until I die. Probably nothing, but you never know. For now, I'm still alive, and I've come to realize that some of the most horrible moments of my life have led to some of the best, so I'm not one for eating up people's melodrama. Just another day to me.

It felt weird leaving my mom and Liz in the house, but it was time for me to get out of there. I had long ago become the man of the house, since no one else was laying down the law, and when my father died that really cemented my status. But I knew if I didn't get out of there soon, I may never get out.

However crazy things got, I could always lose myself down in my room in the basement (walls painted black), reading Ralph Ellison's *Invisible Man* with the headphones over my ears cranking The Who *Live at Leeds* or John Lennon's *Plastic Ono Band* or whatever it was I was into that year. Even at this terrible stage in The Summer of Love, I could transport myself, driving Old Gold and watching the sun go down while I listened to Sly Stone sing "Hot Fun in the Summertime" nice and loud on the shitty cassette deck duct-taped under the dashboard.

I got to Richmond and enrolled in school. I had no interest in school, but everyone else seemed to be doing it and I had no other plans. Because my grades were so bad in high school, due to complete disinterest on my part, I was only accepted on a part-time basis. Felt totally alone and miserable.

One night I was walking past one of the city campus buildings and heard the sound of pianos. I walked in to discover it was the music section of the school. I wasn't interested in studying music that way but was dying to play something, anything. I began sneaking into one of the piano practice rooms every day or night, always worried about being caught, since I wasn't supposed to be there. It was the only time I felt good, banging away on the keys, making up little songs as I went along. Sometimes I'd imagine a lot of people listening to what I was playing, and liking it. One night I got into it so much that I broke one of the big, low piano strings, which made a sound like a shotgun going off. I quickly left the building before I got in trouble.

I was sinking deeper and deeper into despair. I wasn't the least bit interested in any of my classes. My only relief was music. I began to feel what could almost be described as a lust for writing and recording music. I would walk dazed through the streets of Richmond, dreaming of going back to my mother's piano and setting up a tape recorder and microphone.

——

SOME NIGHTS, ALL THESE YEARS LATER, I'LL SIT here and think about when I was really young and how great it felt when things were OK and we were all there in the house: my father reading the paper, Liz playing Neil Young over and over in her room, my mom laughing her goofy laugh at something that wasn't that funny to begin with. When I think about the feeling of being in the middle of that, I'm overwhelmed with desire, like I'd give anything to spend a night back there again.

Life is so full of unpredictable beauty and strange surprises. Sometimes the beauty is too much for me to handle. Do you know that feeling? When something is just too beautiful? When someone says something or writes something or plays something that moves you to the point of tears, maybe even changes you. It's nice when a nonbeliever has to question his doubts. That might be what led me to music in the first place. It was like magic. I could transcend the shitty situations around me and even turn them into something positive just by setting them to music.

Maybe I don't like people as much as the rest of the world seems to. Seems like the human race is in love with itself. What kind of ego do you have to have to think that you were created in God's image? I mean, to invent the idea that God must be like us. Please. As Stanley Kubrick once pointed out, the discovery of more intelligent life some-where other than Earth would be catastrophic to man, sim-ply because we would no longer be able to think of ourselves as the center of the universe. I guess I'm slowly becoming one of those crusty old cranks who thinks animals are better than people. But, occasionally, people will pleasantly surprise me and I'll fall in love with one of them, so go figure.

So what kind of an ego do you have to have to write a book about your life and expect anyone to care? A huge one! But not so big that I think I was created in God's im-age. Unless God is a hairy ectomorph with bad posture (God forbid I don't use the almighty uppercase "G"). And I know I'm not the most famous guy in the world. People aren't making up rumors about gerbils getting stuck up my ass or anything like that. Some people think I've deliberately shot my fame in the foot with some of my "career" decisions, but that's really not the case. I never wanted to be famous for the sake of being famous. I decided to try and make something good in the world, as best as I could anyway, and that was the only goal. So, I only do what I want to do, and I spend a lot of my time on Earth saying "no" to all the stupid things I'm asked to do that I know are a bad idea for me. I'm not a really famous guy, and that's who usually writes books about their lives, but, nonetheless, I've been through some situations and I've decided it's time to write them down. This isn't the story of a famous guy. It's just the story of a guy (who occasionally finds himself in situations that resemble a famous guy's life). There's an inherent ME, I'M SO IMPORTANT thing about doing this that makes me uncomfortable. But I wouldn't do it if I didn't think it happened to be a peculiar story. I'm not so important.

Thanks to my ridiculous, sometimes tragic, and always unsteady upbringing, I was given the gift of bone-crushing insecurity. One thing you'll notice about people with mental problems is the constant self-absorption. I think that's because it's such a struggle just to *be* who they are, so they have a hard time getting past it. I am no exception to this rule. But luckily for me, I found a way to deal with myself and my family by treating it all like a constant and ongoing art project, for you all to enjoy. Enjoy! You're welcome!

Also, judging by my family history, midlife may have been a long time ago for me. So I do feel like maybe I better write this all down now, just in case I don't beat the odds. Don't want to wait too long.

Now, there are different ways I can go about this. I could do it kind of "poetic" for you. Like this:

As I stood there on the porch I noticed the pungent smell of fresh-cut grass and I could hear the faint hum of lawn mowers all over the neighborhood. The air-conditioning poured out on me as I waited. Finally, Mary came down. I never made it inside. She broke up with me right there. I walked home with the cicadas singing, oblivious to my pain.

Or I could turn it up a notch and get really flowery for you. Like this:

In the distance I could hear the faint hum of lawn mowers. Golden, waxen-chested boys, sweating in the sun, a last experience with genuine physical labor before they bundle duffel bags and ship off to Yale or Brown. I could hear Mary's footsteps on the stairs, she hesitates. I notice a cricket—no, it's a grasshopper—at my shoe. I don't know how Mary feels about me, but this little one sees me for who I really am. We connect for a moment and he hops away. I'm alone now. Mary appears. She's going to break up with me, I can see it on her face. She's going to take the unbridled and wholly unconditional love I've offered her and throw it to the ground, shattering it into thousands of tiny, useless shards. I steady myself. I steady myself. (Chapter end.)

Or I could just be straight with you. Like this:

One day in July I went over to Mary's house to hang out for a while. She answered the door but I never even made it inside. She broke up with me on the front porch.

I don't want to waste your time with the flowery shit, so, out of respect for you, gentle reader, I'm going to stick with the direct approach.

I never had an interest in keeping a diary. I had my hands full just trying to live life, so I never kept one. And I didn't feel like I could handle reliving a lot of it. But that's exactly what suddenly appealed to me when my friend Anthony urged me for the thousandth time to write a book about my life. I have this strange mechanism that activates when I think something is off-limits: I know I have to go there. Even if it means painstakingly recalling all the events my selective memory can muster.

In elementary school I was a skinny little kid with long hair who was often mistaken for a girl and was the last, or second to last, to be chosen for school sports teams. Now

I'm a grown man, spending the second half of his first midlife crisis hiding behind security guards that try to protect him from the latest obsessed stalker at his rock concerts. How did I get here?

2

GOOD OLD DAYS/
SHUT UP OR DIE

I WAS BORN THE SON OF A HUMBLE MECHANIC.
A quantum mechanic. My father, Hugh Everett III, author
of the Many Worlds Theory, was a quiet man during the
eighteen or so years I shared a house with him. Turns out
he was depressed over a sad childhood and then being
dismissed as a kook, only later—too late—to be recognized
as a genius. I learned more about him from books and
magazines after he died than I ever could have learned
from the few dozen sentences he uttered to me in those
eighteen or so years in the house.

My dad's father was Col. Hugh Everett Jr., U.S. Army.

He was an imposing figure: tall, cue-ball bald with a neatly trimmed silver goatee beard on his chin. As my grandfather, he was a fun old guy who would take me out to watch the trains come through Berryville, Virginia, where he lived. Occasionally he'd lock my sister and me up in his one-hundred-year-old coat closet, turn out the light, and announce that a ghost named "The Royal Gazunk" was coming to see us. Some might call this terrifying abuse, but I remember it being fun. But back in the 1940s, he made my dad go to military school and my dad hated it. Col. Hugh also insisted on referring to my dad, who was always on the heavy side, as "Pudge." From the time he was a little kid right on through his adulthood, my dad was called "Pudge" by his father. I witnessed this many times. A great esteem-builder. Like calling your one-legged daughter "Stumpy." OK, not that bad, but still—pretty bad.

My dad's mother was Katharine Kennedy, a poet with a history of mental problems. Col. Hugh and Katharine divorced when my dad was only eight, which was not the most common thing back in the 1930s. My dad and his mom didn't have a good relationship and he never really warmed to her.

No wonder "Pudge" never spoke much. He was an only child, way too smart for the regular chimps around him, corresponding with Albert Einstein at the age of thirteen, cooking up unheard-of concepts where anything that can happen in this world *is* happening somewhere, while his crazy mother wasn't much of a part of his life and his army father called him "Pudge." He grew to hate authority.

Katharine spent time in a mental hospital and died not long before I was born. I found a book of her poems in the attic called *Music of Morning*. Here's a sample from a poem called "This Was the Vision," published in 1937, when my father was seven years old:

> *Suddenly there was music:*
> *I listened; I heard*
> *Beneath the cadence something blurred,*
> *Something desperate and far and fierce and sweet*
> *Calling . . .*
> *Something close to the core of Life:*
>
> *I saw Life in mosaic, in motif like roses*
> *Thrown note by note into a Face . . .*
> *Under the chords,*
> *Thrusting at me through the notes*
> *Was something pulsing, something relevant*
> *   to wings and spaces,*
> *Something sweeping and light,*
> *And sure of pattern.*

Col. Hugh thought the best way to raise a child was to let him sink or swim on his own. Literally, in the case of my father. They threw him in the lake so he'd have to learn how to swim. For some reason, my parents decided the sink-or-swim child-rearing theory was a good one for their kids as well. They had no rules for my sister or me. We were expected to learn everything the hard way—by doing. Of course, everyone knows this is a crazy and bad idea now. Kids need adults to lay down some law. Too much law isn't good, but too little law is a whole other ball of wax. If kids aren't able to be kids, then they become little adults during childhood—and then overgrown babies as adults. It's backwards.

In the '50s my father met my mother, Nancy Gore, a pretty, slim, brown-eyed brunette, at Princeton, where he was attending and she was a secretary. She came from Amherst, Massachusetts, the youngest of three children. Her father, Harold Gore, was a college basketball coach and ran a summer camp in Vermont called Camp Najerog, which was my grandmother Jan Gore's name backwards, sort of. He's in the College Basketball Hall of Fame or something.

My mom and dad got married and moved to Alexandria, Virginia. My sister, Liz, was born in 1957. My dad was not into the idea of children whatsoever, so it was up to my mom to deal with anything kid-related. She tried to have another baby a few years later but she miscarried. That's as close as I got to having a dead Elvis twin. I never named it or spent nights talking to it, though.

By the time I came along in 1963, my sister, an impossibly cute little blond girl who could get away with murder, was six and probably already well fucked-up from the sinking and swimming, but mostly sinking. Anything I would do to cause trouble later was not so newsworthy after the shit she was pulling. I learned everything from her.

———

MY EARLIEST MEMORY IS OF FALLING DOWN THE stairs in the little Alexandria house and seeing my father look up from his newspaper. He looked like Orson Welles. The same goatee beard, receded hairline, round head and body. Smoked three packs of Kents a day, always with a little filter cigarette-holder between his eccentrically long-nailed fingers.

When I was two we moved into a new housing development built on old Civil War farmland in McLean, Virginia, an about-to-be rapidly growing suburb just outside of Washington, D.C. My father was now working at the Pentagon as one of Robert McNamara's "whiz kids," as they were then known. His genius at theory having been dismissed after a disastrous summit in Copenhagen, he needed a real job now and the Vietnam War was paying. We had a Teletype machine in the basement that was always humming with printouts from the Pentagon. The basement was also stocked with boxes of freeze-dried food and guns. Not sure what my dad was expecting, but knowing he had a direct connection and felt the need to arm the house for Armageddon didn't exactly help to instill any feelings of security.

It was the mid '60s and everybody was starting to have really whacky ideas. My dad was always a sucker for new ideas and gadgets, so we were always the first to have a new thing, like a microwave oven or VCR. Unfortunately, the first things were also always the worst things. They didn't know how to make them right yet. I still suspect that old behemoth microwave was spewing cancer-causing shit all over the house.

Our house was still being built when we moved in. The housing development was made up of a few prototype model houses, and the prototype of our house had a basement, middle floor, and upstairs. At the back of the middle floor there was a room that homebuyers had the choice of making either a little dance floor/party room or a really small pool. It was a wacky '60s groovy idea and the neighbors with any common sense went for the floor in their houses, but my dad went for the pool, of course, which was tiny and ridiculous and a lot of trouble over the years. We could have used the space for something more practical, but this was not a practical family. We were the weird family on the block, to be sure. There weren't any other dads like my dad. All the other dads played football with their sons, coached Little League, barbecued, etc. Mine sat there.

Living just a few miles from the CIA, our neighbors

were a strange mix of CIA spies, visiting diplomats, and government workers. Then there were the real Virginia people: the rednecks who grew up there and the black community that had lived down the road since the century before. One of the new houses in our neighborhood was built right in front of their church's graveyard, which was full of old gravestones with names like "George Washington" and "Abraham Lincoln" chiseled on them.

Throughout the years we lived together, my dad was a permanent fixture at the dining-room table, scribbling crazy-looking physics notations on yellow legal pads, reading the paper, drinking gin and tonic, and smoking Kents. Then he'd migrate to the living room and watch the news and fall asleep in the same position on the couch every night, with his leg straddling the top of the couch back, so the neighborhood kids looking through the living-room window could tease me about him "humping" the couch. He snored really loud. My mom and Liz would take turns poking him or turning him over so the snoring would stop. But it always came back and all we could do was turn the TV up until you could hear Walter Cronkite a block away.

My father was so uncommunicative that I thought of him the same way that I thought of the furniture. It was just there. The rare times when he became animated were fascinating for me and my sister. It was just so infrequent and unexpected. We had an old Siamese cat named Tut who was sick for years (probably from the microwave) and would make this terrible yelping meow all the time. My dad seemed oblivious to it, like everything else. After a few years of this, a day came where the cat was yelping as usual and my dad finally looked up from the paper and calmly said, "Shut . . . up."

Liz and I looked at each other. The cat continued to whine from the other room and my dad turned up the volume in his voice a little.

"Shut . . . UP."

We were fascinated. He was talking! Something was affecting him! The cat continued yelping. Suddenly, my father's face turned red and he got this crazy look in his eyes, threw his newspaper on the table, screeched his chair back, shot up from the table, and, in a booming, maniacal voice, yelled: "SHUT UP . . . OR DIE!!!!!!!"

Liz and I were delighted by this explosion, partly because it was such a novelty and partly by the pure exotic thrill of seeing the old man emote. "Shut up or die" became a long-standing catchphrase for us after that. We were big on catchphrases. Another favorite was "Where's my goddamn *Newsweek*?!" from another rare outburst. Liz and I were very devoted to the longevity of our catchphrases, some of them lasting several years. Even the way we addressed our parents was a joke. We started calling them "Mother" and "Father" in posh accents for a laugh, and then couldn't stop for years. Finally we switched it to the opposite, "Ma" and "Pa," which we continued to call them for the rest of their lives.

———

WHEN I WAS A LITTLE KID I WAS IN LOVE WITH my mom, and obsessed with her breasts. There, I said it. Years later I would learn in therapy that this admission was actually one of the more normal things about my upbringing. She was very childlike in some ways and seemed to live her life to help others as much as she could. But she was raised by her New England family not to show emotion and could unwittingly be cruel and overly critical. And she was prone to random crying jags that left me feeling helpless. It was tough for me because I needed a mother and, as a result, still do (it's OK, ladies, I know it's not gonna happen, and I'm OK with it). As I grew up, my mom started to feel more like a sister or daughter.

Nothing beats the helpless confusion I would feel on the crying-jag days. Like the day she was vacuuming the living-room floor. I must've been around three or four at the time, just sitting on the floor nearby playing with some Matchbox cars. As far as I could tell nothing happened, but she suddenly turned the vacuum off, threw the nozzle on the floor, and started crying. She ran up the stairs screaming indecipherable words through her tears in a high-pitched squeal that made my ears hurt, slamming the bedroom door behind her. That kind of thing.

But then, a few days later, I tripped over the cord to my new train set that I had just finished setting up, sending the tracks and train cars flying in all directions. I burst into tears and started to run out of the room. My mom ran in from the kitchen and stopped me. In a very tender way, she took my hand and led me back to the dismantled train set, picking up pieces of train track and saying, "Don't worry. This goes here. And this goes here. We'll get it back."

She had a way of looking disapprovingly at me a lot of the time or, if someone liked something I did, she may say something like "what's *wrong* with them?" but she loved me. I mean, really loved me, the best way she knew how. She didn't have a clue how to be a proper mom most of the time, but she definitely loved the hell out of me in her own, crazy way. She made me feel really special, to the point that it's probably been one of my biggest problems ever since. Once you're conditioned for specialness, you don't feel comfortable being not special. She didn't give me the kind of crazy, unconditional love someone like Frank Sinatra's mom gave Frank—you know, that "my son is the greatest" kind of love—there were definitely conditions here, and I wasn't always the greatest in her eyes, but you could tell that I was her little man, you know?

Between her and my father, it didn't feel like there was any secure, sane, authority-like figure of any kind around.

I always felt alone and in charge of my own destiny, whatever little say I had in it. It was a shaky and stressful way for a kid to live. Neither of our parents spoke directly or intimately to us about anything important. Loneliness was instilled.

My parents had some kind of a '70s swinging marriage. I wasn't aware of it at the time. They were good at being discreet. I only knew about it after the fact, when my mom and I had some heart-to-heart discussions later in her life. Who would have guessed that the quiet guy at the dining-room table had a social side, let alone *that*? It must have been past my bedtime. I think it was limited to the occasional affair here and there, on both their parts. But they stayed together until death did they part. It was all very *Ice Storm*. They were trying to be cool and enlightened, I guess. My mom's blue Vega had a "NORML" sticker on it (something about legalizing pot). My dad drove a used Cadillac with a CB radio under its dashboard. His CB "handle" was "Mad Scientist."

One thing I should tell you is that, as a little kid, I had a very hard time with the realization that inanimate objects didn't have feelings and thoughts. I would run it through my head over and over, but I just couldn't grasp that the bathroom cabinet, for example, didn't have feelings and wasn't thinking something at that very moment. I tried to think of it as wood and metal and nothing more, but it just didn't make sense to me. I remember being on the verge of tears, standing there in the bathroom, as my mom tried to make me understand that the bathroom cabinet wasn't going to be hurt if I closed it too hard. I thought of the bathroom cabinet as one of my many friends. Maybe I was confused because I thought of my father as a piece of furniture. I got past this phase around the time I woke up to see my mom sneaking out of my room after leaving the Tooth Fairy's fifty-cent piece under my pillow one night.

I was always busy building and making things. First cities with my Matchbox cars and train tracks, then I started making up little songs on the upright piano my mom brought with her from Massachusetts. I would go door to door inviting the neighbors—and charge them admission—to puppet shows I put on in the living room. I set up my own "radio station" in the basement where I ran a wire upstairs to a shitty RadioShack speaker-cone in the dining room, so the family had to sit there and try to eat while listening to whatever I was spinning and blathering about from the basement with all the fidelity of a loudspeaker announcement from an episode of *M*A*S*H*, which seemed to be a constant presence on the living-room TV set.

When I was six I saw a toy drum set at our next-door neighbor's garage sale. I ran back to our house and begged my parents for the fifteen dollars to buy it. They relented, and began a life of even more noise. I seemed to have a natural knack for drumming and quickly became a good drummer. Everyone seemed impressed. I was always playing in older kids' bands. My identity was Marky, the cute little kid that hung out with the older kids. Now I'm often the oldest guy in my bands, which still feels weird to me after all those years as the youngest.

———

I STARTED OUT ON THE WRONG FOOT AT school, or maybe I should say that school started out on the wrong foot with me. We lived in the closest house to the local public elementary school. Not long after I started walking the short distance to school every day, I became depressed thinking about taking this walk for six more years, and then . . . more school. During my first month in first grade, the teacher—let's call her Mrs. Bitch—accused me of cheating on a math test and humiliated me in front of the class. A first-grade math test: something like, "How many apples are in the barrel—2 or 3?" I was spacing out, looking out the window like I tended to do in order to escape the utter boredom of being there, when the teacher called me up to her desk and announced to the class that Mark Everett was cheating, that he was looking at the next kid's test.

I stood in front of her desk with my legs shaking and told her the truth: I wasn't cheating. I was only looking out the window. I may not have inherited my father's gift for mathematics (indeed, I did eventually flunk out of the easiest ninth-grade algebra class), but I knew how many fucking apples were in the barrel. Adjusting her dark schoolmarm bun, she looked over her cat glasses at me with a piercing grimace and kept ordering me to admit that I had cheated, and I kept denying it.

"Mark, you were cheating. Just admit it."

"I wasn't cheating."

"Come on, Mark. You were cheating. Now admit it."

"I wasn't."

Finally, after five or ten volleys of this, needing an end to the humiliation, I relented and lied, "OK! I was cheating!"

I burst into tears and she dismissed me. As I walked back to my desk and slumped down in my chair, I could tangibly feel my spirit crawl down inside myself to hide.

I continued walking to school every day, but I wasn't the same. Whatever trusting, outgoing side I had seemed to be pretty much gone now. I began living inside myself, going through the motions on the outside. If this was the real world, I didn't like it. What I knew so far: an innocent man can be found guilty. To this day, I have a complex where, if a deed is done and it's a mystery who the culprit is, even though I'm never the culprit, I will nervously feel like I better "act natural" so they don't suspect me, as if I actually am the culprit. Thanks for that, Mrs. Bitch.

I started to look down at the ground a lot. I felt better alone, playing my drums.

At the end of the year there was a first-grade talent show

where I made my show business debut. I played my toy drum set along to a record of "The Star-Spangled Banner." It was an odd choice to rock out to, and a pretty ridiculous scene. In front of the packed elementary school cafeteria, I quickly set up my drums and handed "The Star-Spangled Banner" record to Mrs. Edie, the short, squatty second-grade teacher and talent show MC. She pulled the record from the cover, placed the disc on the little monophonic school record player, and put the needle down. The sound of trombones started blaring an instrumental version of "The Star-Spangled Banner." I looked at my drums and realized I needed a chair to sit on before I could play them. I ran over to Mrs. Edie, who didn't understand what I was asking for.

"A CHAIR! I NEED A CHAIR!"

"Oh . . . you need a chair. Well, all right. Let me see if I can get you a chair."

She waddled over to a cafeteria table and looked around for an empty chair. Finally she motioned for a kid to get out of his chair. She brought it over to me and I quickly threw it behind my toy drum set and tried to pick up in the middle of the song. It was just getting to the part where the lyrics would say, "And the rockets' red glare" and I did a dramatic drum-roll on my tom-tom that started very lightly at the beginning of the line and ended extremely loud with a cymbal crash at the end of the line. The place went crazy. When I was done, the cafeteria erupted in applause.

Thus began the strange parallel universe of my life: hide inside yourself in real life—you'll only be hurt and humiliated—but get on stage and put on a passionate, feeling show, motherfucker.

———

THERE WAS ONE BLACK KID IN MY FIRST-GRADE class and I became friends with him. He lived in the black neighborhood that our housing development was built on top of. I'd go over to the old neighborhood and hang out with him and his family after school a lot. One day I came home and told my parents that I wanted to be black. If there was a way, they would have let me.

In second grade I met a shaggy-haired fat kid named Anthony Cain, who went by "Ant." He was my age and lived on the next street over. I remember the moment I met him. I was pushing my bike up the street and he was standing there in the middle of the street with a group of kids cluttered around him. They were watching him run through his *Let's Make a Deal* TV contestant shtick, slapping his hands on his cheeks like a woman who had just been picked by the host to compete on the show, shrieking "Monty! Monty! Monty!" I liked his style. He was too fat and I was too thin. Like me, he was also often mistaken for a girl, was one of the last to be picked for sports teams, and he had a thing for performing. We formed a bond that's lasted over three decades. He's the guy who urged me to write this book.

One of my favorite mean comments about my physique came when a kid referred to my spindly limbs by saying, "I've seen better arms on a turntable." Kids can be so cruel, but you have to admit, that's a pretty good one.

In third grade some people from the school office came to my classroom and pulled me out of class. As they walked me up to the office I was scared, thinking of all the possible things I'd done that I must now be in trouble for (thanks again, Mrs. Bitch). When I got to the office, they sat me down and told me that I did so well on a recent aptitude test that they weren't sure if I should be there. I wasn't sure if I should be there either, but I was there for another three years, anyway. Sort of.

I was totally bored and disinterested in school throughout my educational career. From the beginning to the end. Hated every moment of it and got bad grades most of the time. I just couldn't be bothered. I hated going to school so much that I began faking sick to get out of going. In fifth grade, I faked sick so much that I missed more school days than I attended that year.

———

ONE OF THE BRIGHT SPOTS IN MY LIFE WAS MY sister, Liz. She was the greatest. Even though I was six years younger, we were really close. She included me in a lot of her activities, letting me hang out with her and the older kids. The activities often included smoking pot, drinking beer, and listening to music. She was skinny and blond and had big tits and everyone wanted to fuck her, and probably did, so there were always plenty of older kids around for me to hang out with and be wrongly influenced by. I loved being part of the older crowd.

We used to have so much fun, me and Liz. Even when I was really little. And she was very protective of me. When the girl next door called me "Retardo," Liz was quick to snap back "Don't call my brother Retardo!" All this kindness while I was doing shit like eating the Pillsbury cookie dough out of the refrigerator, denying to my mother that I ate it, and watching my mom turn around to accuse Liz while I made the "ha-ha" face and stuck my tongue out at Liz behind my mom's back.

Not to mention the Christmas-ball juggling incident. When I was really young, some relative, I don't know who, gave my parents a yellow glass Christmas-tree ball with "LIZ" written on it, and a red one with "MARK" on it. Liz and I came up with the idea that whoever's ball broke first would be the first to die. One holiday season when I was about nine or ten, I was doing my usual funny juggling of the LIZ and MARK Christmas balls, as I did for effect every year, to freak Liz out. She was begging me to stop, as she did every year, saying it wasn't funny and then, yes, the yellow

LIZ ball landed on the outside of my hand. I tried to grab it with my palm but I couldn't get a grip on it. It smashed into pieces on the floor. The MARK ball survives to this day. I wish it had been the MARK ball I dropped that day.

We were almost always having fun in each other's company, but we had our moments like any siblings. Once Liz got mad at me for playing the drums in the house, walked up to me while I was in the middle of playing, and yanked the sticks right out of my hands. She hid the sticks from me and I told her that one day I'd make my own record and title it "NO THANKS TO LIZ."

The other bright spot in my life was music. From the time I got my toy drum set at six, I was always into music. But never what the kids my age were into. The kids at school were listening to "You Light Up My Life" or whatever. I was listening to stuff that Liz was passing down to me. Mostly rock music that was already old. The Beatles had broken up years ago and the music of the mid-1970s was not interesting to me.

John Lennon was on TV a lot, going through his painfully self-conscious hippie routine—the kind of thing that was encouraging whacky *Ice Storm* families like mine. But that *Plastic Ono Band* album he made was really something. Looking back, it seems like a weird record for a ten-year-old kid to love as much as I did—one of the most famous rock stars in the world digging down to the very root of his troubles, shrieking in pain over the loss of his mother—a commercial and critical flop at the time of its release, but it all made sense to me, somehow.

I remember singing a song from that album called "My Mummy's Dead," while I sat in the car as my mom drove around doing errands. "Can't you sing something else?" she would quite reasonably request. I went on to devour all kinds of music, going through intense phases where I wanted to learn everything I could and listen to everything there was of country, soul, oldies, bluegrass . . . it was always changing. One year I was deep into Marvin Gaye, the next year it was Merle Haggard. It wasn't until Prince came along later that I found myself getting into something at the time it was actually happening, instead of something from the past.

The thing I love about John Lennon, and Elvis Presley, for that matter, is that they were really insecure guys and, to me, that's what makes them such thoroughly human artists. No matter how cool they played it, you were still left with the feeling of a real, human experience. Put on any Elvis record, even one of his worst—maybe especially one of his worst—and you can hear his vulnerability just oozing off the grooves. You don't get that from most of the "cool" artists today. They're too busy playing it cool.

———

AROUND THE TIME I WAS TWELVE, A PLANE crashed in our neighborhood. I was alone at home that night, sitting on the vomit-colored carpet in the living room, watching *What's Happening* on TV. A weird orange light started to shine through the curtains. Then I heard an awful droning sound that was getting louder and louder. Suddenly there was a giant sonic explosion. The house shook like a severe earthquake had hit (something I would also experience later in life). The windows were rattling and Tut was screaming. Living so close to Washington, D.C., I figured we were being bombed.

Tut ran upstairs to hide and I ran after him, unsure of what I was doing, my heart pumping wildly. I ran back down the stairs and turned on the CB radio my dad had on the kitchen counter, but then it occurred to me that maybe the house was on fire, so I better get out of it.

I ran out into the street barefoot, trying to figure out, like the TV show I had just been watching, what was, indeed, happening. I ran toward the huge funnel of smoke that was lit up in the night sky by flames and emergency lights, passing seats and ashtrays and body parts that were littered all over the neighborhood. One house had been completely leveled and there was a group of bodies all lying in near proximity by the park. As my bare feet hit the asphalt, I sped up and thought about how these people were just alive but now they were dead, and how much I felt alive at that moment.

3

FIRST GIRLFRIEND

IN SIXTH GRADE THE CLASS TOMBOY TOOK A liking to me. Let's call her Jessie, since she may still be alive and I don't want to embarrass her. We kind of looked the same. Both of us had brown hair, about the same length. She had short hair for a girl, I had long hair for a boy. I was never saying much in class, but she was outgoing and started talking to me on the playground and passing me notes in class. She was the daughter of a congressman. Our first "date" consisted of her teaching me how to play truth or dare in the tree house behind her house one Saturday morning. She told me to pull my pants down and lie on top of her. I couldn't have been happier.

I was totally in love with her and figured we'd get married as soon as we could. I never stopped thinking about her. We would go to the mall, or ice skating, or to the movies, always having a great time. I wrote my first real song on the piano about her, but I never dared play it in front of her. In gym class, when we had to learn square dancing, the teacher automatically paired us up as partners. We were always together. The notes I passed back to her in class got longer, filled with lots of bad schoolboy poetry. We would go down to my room after school, take off all our clothes and get under the covers of my bunk bed's bottom bunk where we'd try to have sex. We didn't know what we were doing, but I loved it. Just being near her, smelling her, touching her, was the greatest thing I'd ever experienced.

This went on for several months, on into the winter. The teacher and all the kids knew we were an "item," but, being only eleven or twelve years old, no one could have imagined how deep I was in it, or that we were taking our clothes off every day after school. I never considered talking to any of the boys in our class about what we were doing. They wouldn't have believed it, or understood what it meant to me, anyway.

One day we were sitting in class while the teacher talked about Alaska and the Hawaiian islands or something. I got a note passed to me that said only:

I WANNA BREAK UP SO I CAN GO OUT WITH
SOMEONE ELSE, OK?

I was blind-sided. My eyes welled-up and it was all I could
do to not start bawling right there in the middle of our ge-
ography lesson. Desperately trying to hold it together, in a
state of shock, I wrote an answer and passed it back:

OK. DO YOU MIND IF I ASK WHO?

The reply informed me in dry, static terms that it was a kid
from another class.

It felt like my life was ending. Finally someone had
brought me out of my shell, but it was all over now. How
was I going to go on? It never occurred to me that I would
have to go back to the way life was before her. I wanted to
feel anything but the terrible pain of losing her. I know
you're probably thinking, "Come on, you were eleven,"
but it was huge to me.

I didn't know how to act around her in class now, making forced smiles and small talk. It was awful. I spent the
cold, cloudy afternoons walking aimlessly through the
neighborhood, pulling my wool hat down over my eyes
while I cried, totally isolated and wanting to die. I felt like
I couldn't talk to anyone about it because they wouldn't
understand the depth of my feelings. Nobody else in our
class even *had* a real girlfriend or boyfriend.

After a month, Jessie broke up with the new boyfriend from another class and immediately got another new boyfriend, this time a kid in our class. I constantly had to be in their presence while they giggled and did cute things with each other, including square dancing together, while I had to be paired up with another square-dancing partner at random. Oh, the pain. The rest of the school year was a long, horrible blur of faked, cordial smiles to the happy couple while I dug a hole deeper inside myself.

The next year I started riding the bus to junior high for seventh grade. I was quiet, still devastated over Jessie, rarely looking up through the long hair covering my face as I walked the halls, a sad sack preteen zombie. I started sleeping late and missing classes. I was so shy and weird that they sent the school psychiatrist to our house to talk to my mother. When the psychiatrist arrived, I crawled out my bedroom window, ran through the backyard, and climbed the tallest pine tree, where I stayed for the rest of the day.

When I walked the school halls, I always kept my eyes down and consciously kept my mouth in a locked, stone-faced position. I did this for so long that my jaw grew from an overbite into a pronounced underbite. I willfully brooded myself into having a severe underbite.

Today I live with the after-effects of all that brooding every day. Not long ago I was standing at a thrift-store counter while the cute cashier girl rang up a friend's purchase. In the middle of opening the cash register, she stopped what she was doing and looked at me.

"Stop making that face," she said.

I wasn't making a face. "What face?" I asked her.

"This one!" she said, as she made a cartoonish, miserable face imitating my underbite.

"Uh . . . that's just my face. Nothing's wrong."

———

TEN YEARS AFTER JESSIE BROKE UP WITH ME, my sister Liz came back from an AA meeting one day and told me that my first girlfriend was now a suicidal, alcoholic lesbian (so much for anonymity, Liz).

4

TROUBLED TEENS

ON THE LAST DAY OF JUNIOR HIGH SCHOOL, the principal exploded with rage and threw me into the bushes. Eighth grade was a completely different story from the year before. Even though I was a good drummer, I was too shy and withdrawn to join the seventh-grade school band. During the summer after seventh grade, I started talking on the CB radio my dad had in the kitchen. One night I talked to a sixteen-year-old girl who went by the "handle" "Strawberry Shortcake" (my handle was "Jumping Jack Flash"—I know). She told me to ride my bike over to her house. When the door opened, there was a beautiful, very developed girl (hey, I was thirteen) with shoulder-length brown hair. I thought it must've been her older sister, but it was her. Way too good for me. But we hit it off and I began a regular routine of riding my bike to her house and sitting in the front seat of her dad's car in the driveway while she gave me lessons on how to French kiss.

"OK, but just a little less tongue, nice and soft. Let's try again . . ."

Having a hot, older girlfriend gave me some confidence, and I consciously made an effort to be more outgoing.

Strawberry Shortcake soon moved to Dale City, which wasn't that far away but may as well have been a million miles away to a thirteen-year-old and his bike. I never saw her again. But with my newfound confidence, I decided I would make an effort to be more outgoing at school. I got a haircut and joined the eighth-grade school band, called "jazz lab," playing trap drums as my first-period class every day. I didn't know how to read music and sometimes I'd put the music upside down on the stand and act like I was following it. But my natural ability was enough that, after the first school concert where we performed a song called "Foxy Funk," which was basically a long, showy drum solo by me with occasional stabs from the horn section, The Prettiest Girl in Junior High decided I was cute.

She was also way out of my league, as they say, with her gorgeous shoulder-length brown hair and amazing figure, but, of course, I fell in love with her hard and fast, oblivious to the heartbreak ahead, even after the devastation of Jessie dumping me and Strawberry Shortcake moving. When The Prettiest Girl in Junior High broke up with me a month later it hurt, but I now had enough confidence to keep it from killing me, even after she told me that she was reading my old love notes aloud to her new boyfriend to laugh at. I shouldn't have taken any of it personally, of course. The revolving door spins fast at that age.

Once The Prettiest Girl in Junior High goes out with you, you're deemed worthy and desirable by the cute girls of junior high, so I had a steady succession of girlfriends the rest of the year. It was amazing. I was a completely different person from a year ago. I was going to cool-kid parties—kids my age, not just my sister's friends. I was hanging out with the cool, trouble-making guys and I became an even better troublemaker myself. Skipping classes, smoking pot on school grounds, playing pranks.

One night me and some of the guys were hanging out in my backyard and we hopped the fence over to my old elementary school, where I spray-painted the words FUCK SCHOOL in big black letters on the white bricks at the school entrance. The next morning parents were dropping their little kids off at "FUCK SCHOOL." It was terrible. It still makes me cringe. My reputation got so bad, so quick, I heard that a kid's mom down the street had said, "That looks like something Mark Everett would do." I hope the statute of limitations has run out, now that I've finally admitted that, indeed, Mark Everett *did* do it.

One of my best friends was a black kid named O'Dell. He was really funny and reminded me a lot of Richard Pryor. He had regular comedy routines that included humping the ground maniacally and telling the story of his two dogs having sex that had to be separated by spraying them with a hose, complete with popping-finger-in-mouth separation sound effect. Whenever my mom gave me and O'Dell a ride somewhere, he'd pull out a Parliament Funkadelic eight-track cartridge from his jacket and slip it into the Vega's eight-track player under the dash.

And so there we were, hanging out by the buses, getting ready to go home on the last day of junior high school. I was just standing there laughing with O'Dell and some of our friends while the principal—let's call him Mr. Bottled-up Rage—a tall, stocky man with thinning black hair and horn-rimmed glasses, was standing among a group of teachers nearby. Suddenly the principal freaked out and ran over to me with his eyes rolling around all cockeyed, screaming, "Why, you little punk!" as he picked me up and threw me into the bushes by the school entrance. It completely took me by surprise, and to this day I'm not sure why he did it. Either he was confused about something or he thought my laughter was directed at him, or maybe my reputation made me a symbol of all that was wrong at the school. It shook me up and physically hurt like hell. I crawled out of the bushes, scraped up badly, brushed off my clothes, and walked back over to O'Dell, whose eyes were popping out of his skull. We got on the bus and went straight to the back and lit a joint. The bus driver kicked us off less than a mile into the drive.

By the time I started high school in September, I was starting to lose my confidence. Over the summer I developed bad acne. Then I got braces. I lost the cute thing the girls discovered with my eighth-grade haircut and showy drum solos. I didn't join the band and there were a lot more kids in high school than junior high, thus a lot more mean kids. And mean kids just make you sad and mean yourself. I started to crawl back in my shell and, if I was outgoing, I was just as likely to be mean as I was to be pleasant. Eighth grade was a weird and wonderful exception to most of my school years. For a brief moment I became kind of popular and had fun, but that was over now.

The bright spots at this point in my life were hanging out with Liz, smoking pot, snorting coke, and drinking beer with her and her friends. And periodically rolling my mom's Vega down the driveway in the middle of the night, starting it up once out of earshot, and joyriding around town, two years before I could legally get a driver's license. Liz moved out of the house and in with a man with a big Charles Manson beard who was twice her age.

I tried to make up for Liz's absence by picking up the

slack and getting really wasted a lot. I'd go to my friends' houses and raid their parents' liquor cabinets before they got home, pouring any alcohol from any bottles together in ways that should never be mixed. Then I'd have to act not wasted while one of my friends' parents gave me a ride home. One night I was in the backseat of a parent's car when I suddenly realized that there was no stopping the fact that I was about to vomit. I had been doing my best during the ride to appear clean and sober. I took the ski hat off my head and threw up into it as quietly as I could, hoping my friend's father sitting at the steering wheel directly in front of me wouldn't catch on. I spent the last part of the ride clutching the ski hat closed, trying not to let any vomit seep through. When I got out of the car I walked into a bush and fell over. I woke up the next morning in Liz's bed with vomit all over my chest. I was glad I didn't drown like Jimi Hendrix.

One day the man with the big Charles Manson beard punched Liz in the face and she moved back in with us.

"*M.E!*" Liz announced upon her arrival back at the house. "I'm back!"

I had a few friends also named Mark, so we would call each other by our initials. I was M.E. Sometimes we'd shorten it to just the last initial. With Liz back in the house, we got back to the important business of corrupting me.

When I was fifteen I went to a Grateful Dead concert that some "dead head" friends were going to. I liked some of the records they were playing. I took acid a few times, which was quite an experience. I can still vividly see the cables on the *Who Are You* poster on my bedroom wall slithering like live snakes the first time I did it. At the fifth Grateful Dead show I went to, some asshole was in my seat and wouldn't get out of it. As I wandered aimlessly through the ridiculous spinning pseudohippie dancers, looking for an abandoned seat, it suddenly dawned on me: you people are phony idiots. I went home and cranked *Quadrophenia*.

Soon thereafter, I was running late for school one morning, as per usual, when I walked through the side door, ready to sprint to my first class, and noticed a kid I knew from gym class with a box of puppies in the hall.

"M.E! You need a puppy, don't you?"

I walked over and looked at the three fuzzy little Labrador puppies in the box.

"These two are taken, but this one still needs a home. She drank some antifreeze, but she's OK."

I picked up the puppy and, of course, fell in love instantly. That's how they get you. He saw a sucker coming and went in for the kill. I named the puppy "Fido," carried her with me all day, and took her home that afternoon. My mom made one of her only authoritarian stands and said there was no way we were keeping the puppy. Fido pooped on my bedroom floor, pooped on Liz's bed, and howled all night. The next morning I saw my mom pick up Fido in the kitchen and nuzzle her nose to Fido's. Despite all the pooping and howling, it was clear at that moment that she was in love with Fido as well.

———

I CONTRASTED THE DAYS OF WALKING THE high-school halls, teeth clenched, staring at the floor, with afternoons and evenings of drugs and booze. The truth is, drugs never really did much for me, but I didn't have any better ideas. Eventually I got caught smoking pot on school grounds and was suspended for a week. Later in the year I got caught in the bushes outside the school, drinking gin that I had stolen from my dad's liquor cabinet and going down on my girlfriend. All before 10 a.m. on a Monday. We brushed the dirt off ourselves, she pulled up her pants, and we were escorted to the principal's office where I was suspended for the second time in ninth grade.

That summer I decided I'd better not press my luck driving underage any more and that I'd just sneak the Vega out one last time. At four in the morning, I was pulled over and arrested for running a red light, driving underage, and stealing the car (even though it was my parents' car).

That same week a kid that I had loaned my jacket to, which had my name written inside the collar, broke into the local community pool center and stole the PA system, leaving my jacket at the scene. The police came to our house and I was arrested, although not guilty of the crime. Good thing Mrs. Bitch conditioned me for this.

Amazingly, both of my court dates were scheduled at the same time on the same day, at different county court-houses (I happened to be in the next county over when I got busted driving). I had to tell one court I couldn't make it because I was due in another court at the same time, which made the idea of me being not guilty of the PA theft hardly convincing. Standing in front of the judge at my car-stealing court date scared the hell out of me. The reality of going to jail, or whatever a fourteen-year-old kid goes to, was terrifying. The judge really scared me with a lot of talk about being sent away, and I had to pay a few hundred dollars' fine, which I made mowing a lot of lawns. Around this time they happened to play the *Scared Straight* docu-mentary on TV where a bunch of juvenile delinquents are taken into a prison while real prisoners scare the shit out of them, telling them they're going to be their bitches, etc., and I have to say, along with the judge, it really helped scare me straight.

Ashamed of the fact that no one else would punish me, I tried to punish myself. I grounded myself, forbidding my-self from going out and doing anything except mowing lawns. I stopped smoking pot and snorting coke, and never did again through the rest of high school, but my reputation was so bad from ninth grade that I constantly had kids asking me where they could score drugs.

I was found not guilty in the community center PA burglary case, but the judge made me write a five-hundred-word essay on how to choose my friends better. Of course, I kept hanging out with these kids for years. I really wasted a lot of time hanging out with the wrong crowd. Some of them were nice guys, but there was nothing but wheel-spinning going on. No wonder I didn't see any future. I would ride around with these guys and play Randy Newman's *Good Old Boys* album on the tape deck. They loved when the song "Rednecks" came on and would sing along to it, but they didn't even get it. They thought it was an anthem:

> *We talk real funny down here*
> *We drink too much and we laugh too loud*
> *We're too dumb to make it in no Northern town*
> *And we're keepin' the niggers down*

O'Dell had moved to Illinois and I was left in the cracker barrel. They weren't tuned in to Randy Newman's irony. They loved the song for all the wrong reasons. They didn't realize that the song was making fun of the white guys. Even though this was Northern Virginia, it was still rampant with racism and this song might as well have been a white supremacist rallying cry to them. They were the guys the song was making fun of.

Then there was the daughter of a suicidal urologist

whom I briefly dated. Things were going nicely until I sang a song for her one night.

"I like your voice," she said, "but sometimes you sing like a nigger."

And sometimes there is a defining moment when you realize that the person you've been riding around with in your car, having dinner with, and making sweet love to isn't the right person for you at all. In this case, this was that moment. I was immediately struck by two thoughts:

1) You are a repulsive, stupid person and I can't wait to get away from you.

And 2) Thanks!

I couldn't help but feel good that this dumb-ass Southern racist had made, in her completely inappropriate and ignorant way, an observation that made me feel some vague assurance that I was on the right path musically.

I should have been hanging out with the gay, artsy kids, or whoever was smarter and thinking differently, but I don't think we really had any, none that I knew of anyway. If only I had spent all that time hanging out with artistically minded people, or someone who could've stimulated my mind a little, at least. But even the notion was totally foreign to me.

When I turned sixteen, I was old enough to legally drive. It was a great day for me because it meant a certain amount of new freedom. I hitchhiked to the DMV, took the test, got my license, and hitchhiked home. I immediately asked to borrow the Vega and went out for a ride. I wasn't going anywhere in particular; I just wanted to feel the freedom rolling beneath me. Within the hour I was pulled over and given my first ticket, this time as a legal driver. The cop had a big laugh over the fact that I had just gotten my license that day and gave me a big, Virginian, "Yew juz got yer license tuh-DAY? Well, happy birth-day! Haw haw!" as he handed me the ticket.

Soon thereafter, a friend of Liz's who worked at the DMV supplied me with the revoked driver's license of an eighteen-year-old guy who looked vaguely like me, so I could use it to buy beer. This worked for a couple of weeks until I absentmindedly handed it to another cop who had pulled me over for speeding while I was taking Fido to the vet.

———

AROUND THIS TIME, I SAW THE BAND'S *LAST Waltz* movie and began to idolize their singing drummer, Levon Helm. I was still in the basement drumming every day but I wanted to sing and be more of a front man. I was stuck behind the drums and there weren't many good role models for singing drummers, but he was great. I began going to his solo shows whenever he came to town and would follow him around and ask him stupid questions (for the record, he was always very patient and extremely nice, no matter how much of a pest I was).

In eleventh grade I fell in love with a country girl named Cathy from the other side of the tracks. We didn't have train tracks, but you know what I mean. She lived down off Route 7. She was short with mousy brown hair, not particularly pretty, but there was something about her that I couldn't get enough of. Then one day my car broke down on the way back from the beach, a couple hundred miles from home. I called Cathy from a pay phone at a gas station on the side of the highway and her little sister let it slip that she was out with another guy. I can still feel the pain of that long day, hitchhiking hundreds of miles home, thinking about my girlfriend out with another man. Good times. She married a biker about a year later.

Back at the house, things had fallen into a long-standing, reliable routine. My father sitting at the dining-room table, smoking, drinking, and snoring through the evening news, and my mother puttering around, trying to get him to stop snoring. No matter what outrageous act Liz or I pulled, nothing ever seemed to register very much with them.

To avoid being in school all day, I spent half of each day of my last two high-school years building houses for school credit, as part of a new program to teach kids "real-world skills." I was a shitty carpenter but I liked being out of the classroom, and at least I was building something, which I always had a thing for, from the little towns I would build with my toy train sets to the songs I started making up.

In twelfth grade I joined a band that played mostly Southern rock and blues, where I was the singing drummer, and we became a popular high-school party band. We were called The A.S.A.P. Blues Band, because three of the four members were in A.S.A.P.—the Alcohol Safety Action Project—which was the program you were forced to take after being arrested for drunk driving in Virginia. I was the one who wasn't in the program, so that made me the designated driver of the group.

One weekend my parents were out of town and I had a gigantic party at our house. Printed up flyers and everything. The band played; it was huge. I woke up on the living-room floor at 5 a.m. the next morning with Fido eating a pile of vomit off the floor that I didn't remember throwing up. The house was trashed. The entire street was trashed. I spent the day cleaning up the neighborhood and the house to the point where, upon my parents' return, they were unaware that a party had occurred. The next day I came home from school and one of the crumpled-up flyers advertising the party had been neatly unfolded and stuck on the refrigerator door with magnets. Fido had found the crumpled paper in a bush and brought it to my mom.

Liz fell in love with a nice guy named Michael who soon joined the army. He got stationed in Honolulu and Liz moved there with him. Several months later he suddenly became a hard-core born-again Christian. Overnight he went from being the nicest guy in the world to the most annoying asshole you could ever hope not to meet. A tough break for Liz. I went to Hawaii and helped her move back to our house. We put Liz's Mazda on a ship to California and I drove it straight from Disneyland to El Paso, Texas, thanks to my one and only experience taking speed, which Liz had given me. I stopped driving when I got to El Paso and my sleep-deprived eyes started to see little green monsters on the side of the highway.

For those keeping score, many years later The Prettiest Girl in Junior High saw a photo of me in a *People* magazine review of one of my records and came to my concert in Washington, D.C. After the show she knocked on the tour-bus door. She was very impressed with me. Not that I hold on to the memory of her reading my love notes for her next boyfriend to laugh at, but it was too little, too late. But who's counting?

5

ELIZABETH ON THE BATHROOM FLOOR/ DAD IN THE TRASH

"*LIZ!*"

"*PHONE!*"

I had just answered the kitchen phone. It was Liz's boyfriend, Robert, calling for her. After I called upstairs for Liz to pick up the phone, I heard my mom knock on Liz's bedroom door. Then she knocked on the bathroom door. When no one answered, she opened the door. Then she turned around and called down to me, in a calm voice: "She's asleep."

Pause.

I'm thinking: it's three in the afternoon, why is she asleep?

"On the bathroom floor," my mom says.

I dropped the phone and ran up the stairs, shouting, "Doesn't that seem odd to you?!"

I found Liz, indeed, asleep on the blue-and-white tiles of the bathroom floor, having just ingested a bottle of pills, the empty bottle lying on the floor next to her with the lid nearby. I yelled at her to wake up, slapped her face, peeled her eyes open, yelled again, right up against her ear. Nothing. I ordered my mom to call an ambulance.

The paramedics came quickly and ran up the stairs to try all the same stuff I had already tried. I don't know where I learned all that stuff. Must have been from watching TV. They carried her downstairs and laid her on the carpet by the front door, ripped her shirt off, and tried to revive her some more. The neighbors were all starting to gather on the front porch, looking through the window, trying to see what was going on. A paramedic wheeled in a stretcher and they lifted Liz onto it. Me and my mom got in her car and followed the ambulance to the hospital.

As we entered the emergency room, I saw my friend Anthony sitting there, coincidentally, waiting for poison oak treatment. "Is that Liz?" he asked, looking at the unconscious blond woman being wheeled by on a stretcher.

"Yeah," I said.

As they wheeled her into the emergency room, her heart stopped. They went into "code blue" mode, or whatever you call it, and started to resuscitate her. Amazingly, they revived her. One minute later and she would have died.

—

BACK AT THE HOUSE THAT NIGHT, MY DAD looked up from his paper and said, "I didn't know she was so sad." Liz had been losing it for a while now. She was growing increasingly erratic. She used to be so great when we were younger, and she was so nice to me. I remember the day after I saw the movie *Young Frankenstein*, when I was about ten, Liz drove me to the beach and I acted out the entire film for her during the four-hour drive. It must have been utterly painful and boring for her to sit through, but she acted interested the whole time.

But, as the years went on, she became a bad alcoholic, the kind that always had a beer in her hand first thing in the morning, and the kind whose personality changes greatly when drinking, and not in a pleasant way. Then she started getting into heroin and God knows what else. On top of all that, she started to go crazy. A lot of the time she just wasn't herself and I started to not like her more often than like her. I was becoming the authority figure of the house even though I was the youngest member of the family, eighteen or nineteen at the time. When Liz's desk caught on fire during a party in her room one night, I was the one it was kept secret from. "Don't let M.E. find out about the fire . . ." Eventually I discovered her burned desk and read her the riot act.

One night a few weeks earlier, me, my friend Anthony, Liz, and Liz's boyfriend Robert had just come back to our house after a concert. Robert had a mustache and a Camaro. He was a nice guy, though. We were standing in front of Robert's car, parked in front of our next-door neighbor's house. I don't remember exactly what it was about but Robert was suddenly acting like a total asshole, really out of character. He was giving Liz shit about something and it was getting out of hand. I told him to shut the fuck up and he said, "Oh yeah?" and pushed me to the ground. We were rolling around on the neighbor's grass, punching each other. Liz and Anthony eventually broke it up and pulled us off each other. We cooled off and shook hands, but he still had a weird, out-of-character look in his eyes. Like he was possessed or something.

We all walked over to our house to have a beer. As we walked into the kitchen, Robert suddenly got an even more insane look in his eyes, ran over to the stove and grabbed a butcher knife. He got into a combat stance and then came at me with the butcher knife. It was fucking scary. We were on the kitchen floor, rolling around while he tried to stab me. I was pushing him away with all my might, trying to keep the knife from going in me. Liz was screaming.

Anthony called the cops from the kitchen phone, nice and loud so Robert could hear it. Robert dropped the knife and took off, leaving the front door open behind him. The cops scoured the neighborhood looking for him, but he was nowhere to be found. Later he was evaluated as having a severe personality disorder caused by sleep deprivation, due to his night job.

———

I HAD JUST BARELY GRADUATED HIGH SCHOOL. It was down to the wire, but in the end they let me go. I didn't know what to do, so I figured I better start working. I worked at a print shop run by a crazy old alcoholic asshole who was the father of a friend of mine. One day I couldn't take it anymore. He started some shit with me and I punched my time card out and never came back.

I went to work at the CIA Exxon gas station. This turned out to be a pretty great job. Lots of time to think. I liked pumping gas, cleaning windshields, and changing tires. It was peaceful and most of the customers were nice and pleasant to deal with, although I almost got fired once when this kid who pulled his Trans Am up to the self-serve pump all the time drove in one day and, after he filled up his tank and I cleared the pump, as was normal practice, he snapped at me, in his whiny teenager voice: "Tha-anks! Now I don't know how many gal-lons I got!"

I replied, "Six point se-ven!" mocking his whiny complaint.

He ran into the office and told the station manager what I did and said, "Someday someone's gonna punch that guy in the mouth." I got chewed out by the boss, but he was nice enough not to fire me. Told me not to mock any more customers.

I also worked at a stable, shoveling horse shit and cleaning stalls. I liked it. Plenty of thinking time to sort out my thoughts and lots of pretty girls around with their horses. No one wanted to fire me and I didn't want to quit. It was a lot better than the job I had in the winter, diving into freezing pools to unplug and drain them.

Liz came home from the hospital. She and my mom went on a trip to visit our cousins in North Carolina. One night I was doing the dishes and my dad came in the kitchen and struck up a rare conversation.

"*You're* doing the dishes?" he asked incredulously.

"Yeah, someone's gotta do them," I answered.

"Oh, you're a redneck now, I forgot," he said.

I had recently started doing an old country music radio show out in Warrenton with a friend of mine, Ed, every Sunday night. The good kind of country music, not the money music it is today. We played lots of bluegrass records, Merle Haggard, Willie Nelson, Buck Owens, that sort of stuff. My dad loved "Rocky Top" so I'd play that record a lot. It was great talking to him. I had recently discovered poker and that was the one thing we ever talked about. Occasionally I would even make a late-night call to him for poker advice.

We joked around a little and I remember thinking that it was the most human, real conversation I'd ever had with him. He even told me a joke. An hour later I went out to meet my friends Anthony and Sean to go eat Mexican food. As I walked out the front door, I thought I saw something strange in my peripheral vision: my father lying on the couch, as he always did after watching the news, but backward—with his feet where his head usually was—which would have been highly unusual, something I had never seen. But I was late and as I hurried out the door, I decided that I must have imagined it and kept going.

I came home a few hours later and my dad had gone to bed. I sat in the living room and watched a *Saturday Night Live* rerun with Charles Grodin hosting. I laughed out loud during his Art Garfunkel impersonation. Then I went downstairs to bed.

I woke up early the next morning so I could make the two-hour drive to register for fall classes in Richmond, but something didn't seem right. I don't know how I knew, but I could tell something was wrong.

I went upstairs and the usual signs of my father going to work were not there. No lights were on and it was eerily quiet. I ran up to my parents' bedroom, trying to mentally prepare myself for the worst-case scenario. As I walked in the room, I saw what I was afraid I would see: my father, lying there faceup on the bed, sideways, fully clothed, on top of the covers with his legs bent and his feet almost on the floor.

I thought maybe he fell asleep like that. I said, "Dad? Are you awake?" He didn't respond. I started to panic.

I yelled, "Dad! Wake up! Come on!"

I shook him. "Shit! Come on!"

I yelled right up against his ear, the same way I did with Liz. Just the fact that I was touching him was surreal. I grabbed the phone and dialed 911. When the operator answered I told her that my father wouldn't wake up. She asked where he was and I told her on the bed. She told me to pick him up and carry him to the floor so she could instruct me in CPR. I put the phone down, pushed my arms under his body, and picked him up. His entire body was completely stiff, like a board. I carefully carried him across the room, his body frozen in the position that he was in on the bed, and lowered him to the floor. I put the phone back to my ear and told the 911 operator that his body was stiff and asked her what to do next. She said, "Oh . . . well . . . um, just wait there. Someone will be there soon."

As she finished the sentence I heard sirens blaring in the distance. He must have died the night before. The 911 operator knew there was nothing to do after I told her his body was stiff. The ambulance came and they checked him out. They put a sheet over him and told me to go downstairs. He was only fifty-one. I was in shock and didn't know what to do. It was hard to know even how to feel. My father had just died, but I barely had a relationship with him. And here I was, alone with him in the house, just the two of us. Only, he was dead.

A police officer stood against the wall behind me while I sat at the dining-room table and flipped through a copy of *Newsweek*, crying. The worst part of it all was watching them put my father in a black bag, zip it up, and carry him out through the front door inside it. They didn't put him on a stretcher. They just carried out this black bag, sagging like a sack of trash. I've never been able to shake the images of my father walking into his house one night and then being carried out in a black bag the next day.

I was also haunted by the feeling that maybe I could have saved him if I had paid better attention the night before. Did I really see him facing the wrong way on the couch? Maybe he had started to feel weird then, but made it upstairs and then the heart attack hit him as he sat down on the bed. What if I could have saved him if I had just paid more attention to what was going on there?

I called my mom and Liz to tell them. It was pretty hard telling my mother that her husband was dead. Liz took it the worst. She still called him "Daddy" sometimes. I heard my mom on the other end of the phone tell Liz to sit down. A few moments later I heard Liz scream.

Liz and my mom drove back later that day from North Carolina. That night the three of us all slept in my parents' bed. Liz and I were concerned that it would be too much for my mom to handle losing her husband and suddenly be alone in their bedroom, but she seemed to handle it pretty well. But you could never really tell how anyone was handling anything in this house.

A few days later my mom came back from the morgue with a small bag that contained my dad's wallet, watch, and wedding ring. My dad, who was a devout atheist, had once told my mom that he wanted his remains to be thrown out in the trash. My mom kept his ashes in a box inside a filing cabinet drawer in the dining room for a few years, and eventually honored his request.

6

SODA JERK

MY COLLEGE CAREER WAS MERELY AN EXTEN-
sion of the wheel-spinning I had perfected in high school.
I probably wouldn't have been such a late bloomer, artistically speaking, if I hadn't wasted so much time wandering
through scenes I didn't belong in. I was living in a tiny,
yellow-walled room with two little cots in a shitty high-
rise dorm building in Richmond, Virginia, with my roommate, a black guy named Scrappy (I'm not making this
up). Scrappy was a really nice guy and a great roommate,
but that room was awfully small. About the size of a jail
cell. I got a job as a soda jerk at the school cafeteria. I'd
proudly polish and refill the coffeemakers and soft drink

fountains that I was in charge of every night. Occasionally I would get demoted to dishwasher. Being the only white dishwasher, the other dishwashers ignored me. I'd scrub the dishes coming through on the conveyor belt as fast as I could with my bulky rubber gloves, listening to the radio while one of the other dishwashers, "Babysteps," would sometimes show the others why he was called Babysteps by taking off his rubber gloves, stepping through the cloud of steam, and demonstrating his hallmark dance of very little foot movement, which resembled, yes, baby steps.

There were so many miserable moments, it's hard to pick any out of the long blur of misery held in my memory banks. My dad had just died, I left my mom and sister alone back home, I was living in a strange city I didn't know, going to school, which I didn't care about. I lost my identity as the town singing drummer. It was just a big, depressing blur.

I have random memories, like, one rainy day being in some physical education class I had to take where I was paired up with the hottest girl in the class to do some self-defense moves. I had dreamed about this girl. Thought of what it would be like if I was a lot cooler and had the nerve to ask her out. Even ran through a whole fantasy sequence in my mind where I borrowed my friend George's truck so I could take her out to dinner. So now I was in the gym, lying on top of her in some judo hold we had just been taught, when she looked at the ceiling and said: "Is there a leak in the roof?"

I looked down at her and saw drops of water splashing onto her beautiful face. Then she said, "Oh! It's just . . . um . . . you."

I was dripping sweat all over her face. I apologized, got off her, turned around, and then she screamed, "*OH MY GOD! ARE YOU OK?*"

I turned back around to face her.

"Yeah. What?" I asked.

As other students started crowding around and pointing at my back, she informed me that there was a large pool of blood soaking through the back of my white sweatshirt.

I walked the six blocks back to the dorm with blood spewing out of the giant acne volcano that had burst, one of many now fertilely sprouting on my back, while passerbys on the street pointed to my increasingly blood-soaked sweatshirt and said things like: "Whoa, man! You're bleeding!"

And, "Somebody fucked that motherfucker up!"

"Thanks, I know . . ."

———

I STARTED THE ODD PRACTICE OF JUMPING OUT of planes. Having a general fear of heights, I'm not sure what inspired me to go skydiving. I think it was a combination of wanting to face my fears and wanting to do something that would make me feel alive, not just some walking zombie passing time on Earth. There was a place nearby where you could be trained in the morning and then actually jump out of a plane in the afternoon. I don't know how I got myself to step out onto the wheel of the plane and hang off the strut of the wing with my feet flailing behind me as I looked down on the Earth thousands of feet below. Once I let go, got past the horror of free-falling and the parachute opened, it was the most peaceful and spectacular ride down. I did it a few more times and then wrote a research paper on skydiving where I learned some disturbing facts. A lot more people were dying from it than I thought. I found several skydiving death reports that ended with: *"Cause of death: impact."*

I decided to retire from skydiving.

After that, all I ever thought about was music and how much I missed being in a band and how badly I wanted to write and record songs. But I never thought I could be anything more than the big fish in the small local pond of my hometown that I had already been. I never considered actually trying to make music my life.

I started catching rides two hours north to my mom's house to make little two-track reel-to-reel tapes on the weekends. That summer I bought a used four-track cassette machine from the guitar player in my old high-school band and began obsessively writing and recording songs on it, playing my mom's piano and my sister's acoustic guitar. I didn't bother going back to Richmond.

Over the summer I had a girlfriend, Kim, who lived way out in the country, an hour away. She was a sweet and fun-loving, if not somewhat troubled, girl with brown hair and pretty eyes whom I met through friends at school. I would play her my little tapes and she would encourage me and tell me I should try to do something with my music, but I couldn't imagine anything happening with it other than the joy of making it.

Things continued to get grimmer for Liz. One night she got really wasted and ended up being raped by a group of men she met at an ATM machine. As if all her other problems weren't enough. Between the rape and her constant drinking, she was sinking fast. The men who raped her were black and the trauma turned her into a racist. She started to talk like a stupid, drunk, Southern cracker, which pretty much took away the last of her dwindling charm. Of course, I felt horrible for what she had been through, and was trying to console her, but as time went on, instead of healing, she just got ugly.

At this point, my dream was to have my own tow truck. In my reality, it seemed like a great situation. I'd be my own boss, have my own hours, lots of time to think and sort my thoughts out. I had a little experience with roadside assistance from the gas stations I'd worked at and I liked it. I tried to talk a friend of mine into being my tow truck partner, we could share the truck in shifts, but he never really took to the idea.

I tried to go to school again, enrolling at the state university not far from my mom's house. Once again, I got a job as soda jerk in the school cafeteria. I would sample all the beverages I was in charge of from night to night and tried coffee for the first time, getting hooked in the process. I noticed that I always went to work in a bad mood but came back from work in a good mood and eventually traced the origin of the good mood to coffee.

I quit school again and devoted as much time as I could to writing and recording my four-track tapes. In addition to my drums, my mom's piano, and my sister's guitar, I bought a primitive synthesizer and drum machine at the local music store. I didn't have a goal. I just had a real hunger to make songs. They were about all sorts of things. Some were about girls I liked. Some were about how lonely I felt. The usual song fodder, I suppose. Some were about my questions of what life is all about, or supposed to be about. Musically, they were a weird, naive mix of pop, country, and soul with synthesizer and drum machine. Every week or so I had made a new "album" of songs. I gave the cassettes album titles and then moved on to the next. Sometimes these albums would have an overall "concept" to them, like the one I made about the local black community, full of corny, politically correct lyrics and all.

I worked a lot of odd jobs and bought a blue pickup truck

to start "Mr. E's Hauling Service" so I could make a few bucks hauling people's junk to the dump. My mom made flyers for me and I walked around the neighborhood putting them on people's doorsteps. They soon started calling Mr. E to clean out their attics and haul their junk to the dump. I got a job delivering flowers in a van for the local florist. One day I slipped one flower out of every bouquet I was delivering and made a hodgepodge bouquet, wrapped in a flyer for a band I started playing in, and delivered it to a girl with one leg shorter than the other, who I had an impossibly huge crush on. No one noticed the missing flowers in their bouquets and the girl loved her bouquet.

I never did anything except work, drink coffee, and write and record songs. I had no social life to speak of at this point. Kim had broken up with me twice and, although the other girl liked her bouquet, it wasn't enough. I got a job as a music teacher's assistant at a county school for emotionally disturbed high-school kids. I liked that job a lot. I was good at it and it made me feel good. I had a different band of emotionally disturbed kids (something that would prepare me for the emotionally disturbed band members I would later have to deal with) for each class period, five bands a day. I would play different instruments in each band. Sometimes drums, sometimes guitar, sometimes keyboard. One of the kids was a big Led Zeppelin fan and I gave him John Bonham's drumstick, which I got at the Led Zeppelin concert Liz took me to in eighth grade. A nice gesture, but foolish. I want it back! It had his name on it. Probably worth a lot on eBay now. The kid probably traded it for an ounce of weed the next day.

I was recommended to another school for disturbed kids, this time elementary-school age, and I was good at that, too. It was helping me come out of my shell and I liked the kids. I also worked as a substitute teacher at regular schools. The irony of the kid who hated school so much now being in a position of authority at school appealed to me. That device I have when I feel something is off-limits to me always kicks in and then I have to do it. It could alternately be fun or nightmarish. Like the out-of-control seventh-grade science class: kids all screaming, running around, their Bunsen burners shooting flames. I couldn't deal with it. I sent a kid to the teacher's lounge to get me a cup of coffee and he came back with a note from the principal for *me* to come see him. Apparently you don't send kids to get you coffee. I was still being sent to the principal's office after all these years.

I developed an irrational and embarrassing crush on a girl who worked at the post office. I only ever made small talk with her while buying stamps or sending mail at her counter, but I was always thinking about her. After months of this, I got the nerve to ask her out. She went out with me the day the space shuttle exploded and let me know that she was engaged. I went home and wrote a song called

"The Girl at the Post Office Is Getting Married" and that was that.

I was twenty-three, extremely isolated, and getting sick of my life, or lack thereof. One summer evening I sat on my mom's back porch and felt such a deep emptiness inside me. I felt like such a lost cause, with nothing going for myself. Something suddenly snapped inside me: since I'm such a lost cause, what do I have to lose? Before I just give up and die, I need to at least *try* to do something—and I need to get the fuck out of this suburban wasteland and go on some kind of adventure.

For the first time I started to think about the future. I looked around and didn't see it in my mom's house. I thought about what Kim had said, that I was good at music and should try to do something with it. Why shouldn't I, since it was the only thing I cared about and wanted to do? I decided on the spot that I was going to move somewhere and try to start some kind of new life.

I thought I should go to either New York or Los Angeles if I wanted to do something with my music. I didn't have a clue about either city and didn't know anyone in either of them. I picked Los Angeles because it was farther away and I really wanted to get away. Three thousand miles away.

I started working as much as I could to save up money for the move. By day I was bossing around kids in school, who then took it out on me at night while I trained to be a busboy in hopes of becoming a waiter. Having fifteen-year-olds order you around is a humbling experience. Eventually I was promoted to waiter, which I was really bad at. One night, during the peak of the Iran–Contra scandal, I waited on Oliver North and his family. I was surprised at what a pleasant customer and good tipper he was. But I had to wonder whether my tip had also been diverted from some government fund.

Another night, my mom brought our visiting cousins in and I waited on them. I think she was prouder of me being a waiter than anything else she might have been proud of before or since. After they left, my mom called me at the restaurant, sounding distressed. They were driving near the house Liz had recently moved into with her new boyfriend and saw the winter night-sky lit up by the red lights of half a dozen ambulances and fire trucks on the dirt road leading up to Liz's place, but the road was too snowy for them to get close enough to see what was going on. I threw my apron off and drove over as fast as I could, trying not to lose control of Old Gold on the twisty, icy road, repeating, "No, Liz, no, Liz," over and over to myself. I could see the sky glowing red as I approached Liz's road. I got out of the car and ran to the first ambulance at the bottom of the hill and was told by a paramedic that the house next door to Liz's place had caught fire. I drove back to the restaurant feeling relieved that Liz hadn't killed herself.

After a few months of working two jobs, and selling my drums, I had saved up a decent amount of money. I loaded up everything I owned into my car early one morning. My mom walked out to the driveway and said it felt like her son was going off to war. I got on the highway, not having any idea what I was in store for and not knowing a single soul in California.

7

HOPE YA LIKE STARVIN'

BOB DYLAN SAID THAT, WHEN HE WAS YOUNG, he had a secret sense of his destiny. I wish I had something like that, but I didn't. At all. All I had was an aching sense of desperation and an acute cluelessness—a nasty combination. I didn't have any idea what the hell I was doing and was only doing it out of not knowing what else to do. Music was the only thing I had a passion for and the passion was getting stronger all the time. But I didn't have any idea what could become of it.

I was a real desperate case because it seemed to me that my choices were: give up and die, or: put your blinders on and make something out of all this passion. I put a lot of pressure on myself when I chose to try to make something happen with my music, because I felt like there was nothing else for me. It was literally do or die.

Driving across America with my guitar, four-track recorder, and everything I owned in the car was exciting. It felt like I could pull over at any exit and start a new life if I wanted. Even navigating through a terrible ice storm in Oklahoma felt exciting after so many years of wasting away back home. When I finally got to California, I got the phone number of a sister of my first girlfriend, who lived a couple of hours south of Los Angeles. I called her and she was kind enough to let me sleep on her couch, which turned into a month of sleeping on her couch. Or trying to sleep, since it was difficult getting any rest while her and her boyfriend's loud sexual grunts and screams from the next room echoed through the heater vent every night.

One day I drove up to Hollywood and I couldn't believe my eyes. Growing up watching a lot of TV in Virginia, Hollywood was a mythical place to me. As I exited the 101 freeway, I could hardly contain my excitement at seeing the Capitol Records building right there in front of me. I pulled onto Vine Street and noticed a crowd of people on the sidewalk near the tall building built to resemble a stack of records. I parked and walked over to see what was going on. The actress Angie Dickinson was presenting the band Billy Vera and The Beaters with a star on the Hollywood Walk of Fame. They had just had a big hit song from the TV show *Family Ties*. I watched, transfixed, as Angie Dickinson uncovered the star and stepped aside. While Billy Vera made his acceptance speech, Angie Dickinson walked a few steps over the sidewalk and was now standing right next to me. I had been in town for one minute and I was already standing next to a living, breathing movie star!

My voice cracking, I introduced myself to Angie Dickinson: "Huh-hi, um, Ms. Dickinson, my name is Mark Everett."

Angie Dickinson peered over her gigantic designer sunglasses.

"Nice to meet you, Mark, I'm Angie. What do you do?"

"Uh, huh, um . . . I'm a songwriter."

She smiled.

"Oh, great! I love music. That's why I'm here. What are your songs like?"

I reached into my jacket pocket and handed her a cassette of my latest "album" of four-track songs. She smiled and said she'd listen to it. A hipster-looking guy with an earring standing next to her leaned over to me and said, "Angie's a great person to have on your side."

———

WHEN I WAS GETTING READY TO LEAVE VIRGINIA, I was getting a lot of comments from musician friends along the lines of "Hope ya like starvin'!" That one came from a guy I knew who was a great guitarist in Virginia who had gone to LA to try to make it, but eventually came back dejected. I couldn't believe my luck. It was all so easy. Just drive into town, meet a movie star, and wait for the phone call that informs you that fame and fortune are now yours. Whenever I came back to the apartment I'd immediately ask, "Anyone call for me?" But no one ever did, of course.

Eventually I moved into a crappy little apartment across from the Burbank airport. Moving in across from an airport was a stupid idea on many levels. I never forgot what it sounded like when the plane crashed in my neighborhood when I was a kid. On at least three occasions when planes were landing too close to the apartment, I got down on the floor into crash position.

I only knew Burbank from Johnny Carson always joking about it on *The Tonight Show*. One of the first things I did was go to NBC and stand in line to watch a taping of the show. After standing in line all day, I was almost at the front when they announced that it was full and for the rest of us to go home. As I was starting to walk away, an NBC usher in a blue suit yelled out, "Anyone here alone?" I raised my hand and he gestured for me to follow him. He took me inside the studio and to an empty seat in the center of the fourth row. Having watched the show all those years in Virginia, this was a remarkable experience for me to be on the actual set and see Doc Severinsen warming up the band. Suddenly the band kicked into the theme song, Ed McMahon said "And heeeeerrrre's JOHNNNYYY!" and then I was sitting mere feet away from the great Johnny Carson. I don't remember who else was on the show that night, only the otherworldly thrill of sitting directly in front of Johnny Carson in the flesh.

Soon after that I was standing in line at the post office one day when a big, black limousine pulled up. The door opened and out stepped Little Richard, who got in line next to me. Once again, a totally surreal experience for a kid from Virginia. Little Richard is waiting in line at the post office like a regular person—right next to me! He was wearing a long purple trench coat and was made up like he was on stage. I nervously told him I was a fan of his work and he couldn't have been nicer. He even had God personally bless me.

I set up my four-track recorder in my closet and got back to work. Whenever I wasn't working one of the many jobs I hated, I was feverishly writing and recording in the closet. I bought an old Fender Rhodes electric piano at a yard sale and it became a new part of my four-track sound.

I started sending my tapes to record companies and amassed quite a collection of rejection letters. Every rejection was a crushing blow. Yet, somehow, I kept going. Probably by using the rejection as fuel for my fire. Or, more likely, sheer desperation kept me going. It was the late 1980s, a terrible time to be around music in LA. A lot of hairspray and bad heavy metal. No one was interested in this odd guy from Virginia making weird little four-track tapes in his closet. What I was doing had nothing to do with anything that was "happening." But I never forgot what I learned when I read Ray Charles's book *Brother Ray* when I was a teenager. He said you have to find that thing that's unique about *you*. And that was the mission I was on. To keep whittling away until whatever it was that I had that was uniquely mine really started to shine.

Besides, I hadn't given myself any other choice, so I just kept going. But it was not an easy time. Angie Dickinson still hadn't called and I was only getting rejection, no encouragement whatsoever. I got a job washing cars at a mechanic's garage, across from the high-rise building where PolyGram Records was. I would stand there with the hose in my hand and look up at the building with reverence, like it was a monument. Sometimes I'd ride with the boss over to the other garage he owned across town and he seemed to get into some traffic altercation every time, often pulling a pistol out of the glove compartment in front of me and waving and aiming it at other motorists.

One Sunday morning I bought a bicycle at a Burbank bike shop and rode around town for a couple of hours. It felt great whizzing around and not worrying about anything for once. I could go anywhere and do anything—it was Sunday and I wasn't going to think about how lonely and difficult my life was. I rode by a movie theater and decided to see a movie. I locked up my brand-new bike on the bike rack and went inside. Two hours later I came out and my bike was gone. I had owned it for exactly five hours. It took me months to save up enough to buy another bike.

I would answer ads in papers looking for singers or songwriters. No one ever seemed to know what to make of me. It just wasn't adding up. I'd play one of my four-track songs to some guy from a want ad and he'd say something about how "uncommercial" it sounded. I'd go back to my sweltering apartment and lie on the mattress on the floor, listening to Bob Dylan, the man with the secret sense of destiny, singing "Sign on the Window" on the boom box while I cried and thought about giving up and dying.

My one minute in Hollywood stretched to three miserable years of crappy soul-sucking jobs and dark depression. Thank God I had my songs to write and record. I had no social life whatsoever, just work and record, work and record. Day in, day out. That's all I did.

After a year living across from the airport, I moved to a tiny apartment over a garage in Atwater Village, beside the 5 freeway and the LA "River" (actually a graffiti-riddled aqueduct often used for the dumping of gang-related murder victims' bodies). I got a job answering phones for a local music magazine that existed primarily for the "musicians seeking musicians" want ads in the back. When you called the number to leave your want ad, I was the voice on the answering machine walking you through the steps of placing it. Sometimes I'd even write reviews for the magazine, but that paid worse than answering the phones. Some of the writers would take me along with them to music industry functions and I started to meet more people involved with music, but, as usual, no one was interested in my songs.

One night I tagged along to what turned out to be a record-release party for Fleetwood Mac's Stevie Nicks at some mansion, way up on a hill. I was totally bored and uncomfortable, as I always was at these kinds of things. They weren't glamorous or exciting like I'd imagined. They were dull and full of phony people that depressed me. I went to leave and got in the shuttle van that takes you back down the hill. The man sitting next to me was asking the shuttle driver to change the radio station because he hated the song that was playing. He was an older man with graying hair who kind of reminded me of Albert Finney. I seconded the motion to change the radio station. We chatted a little and I learned that he was John Carter, an A&R man from Atlantic Records and a longtime music business veteran whose first big break was writing the lyrics to the psychedelic sixties hit "Incense and Peppermints." I told him I was a songwriter and, knowing what would happen next, he instinctively put his open hand out. I pulled my latest collection of four-track songs out of my jacket and put the tape in his hand (I later learned that this act is known as "The Nashville Handshake"). I always had a tape on me, usually of something I had just finished that morning, and this one was now set free from my pocket.

The next morning I went out to the store before work. I brought my groceries home and saw the red light blinking on my answering machine. I pressed the playback button and took a carton of eggs out of the grocery bag. As I put the eggs in the refrigerator, the message played: *"E, it's Carter. Great songs, great lyrics, great melodies. We'll talk."* Click.

No number for me to call back, just "we'll talk."

8

GARAGE SALE

I CALLED INFORMATION AND ASKED FOR THE number for Atlantic Records. I got through to John Carter's secretary. I explained that I had gotten a cryptic but encouraging message from her boss. She said the cryptic thing was typical. I wasn't sure how typical the encouraging part was. Did he mean business? She put me through to him and, indeed, he said he wanted to sign me to Atlantic Records.

This was too good to be true. Was my life going to have some purpose after all? Would I be able to actually do something with my songs? Would I even be *paid* to write and sing my songs? I was extremely excited.

Weeks went by and my excitement dwindled as I heard nothing more from Carter. Eventually I called him and he told me that he had presented my tape to the head of Atlantic but he didn't like it, it was too odd, so that was that. I was crushed. I was used to rejection, but not being rejected after thinking I was *in*. I didn't realize there was another step for approval. I figured that Carter saying he wanted to sign me was the end of the story.

Although completely disillusioned, I went back to my usual routine of working and feverishly writing and recording songs. No matter how much rejection I faced, I kept writing and recording because I had some unspeakable need to do it. I just kept doing it, even if no one was ever going to hear it, I loved doing it. But I did want to communicate to people and I wasn't very good at it outside of a song, so it was still important to me to try to be heard.

Carter gave me his home number and told me to keep in touch. One day soon after, I was at the magazine office, washing the boss's coffee mug out in the men's bathroom, when I overheard the boss say that Carter had been fired from Atlantic Records.

I called Carter and asked him what he was going to do now. He said he wasn't sure and asked if I had any new music. I told him I always had new music. I rode my bicycle over to his house in Silver Lake and dropped off a tape of some new songs. He left another encouraging message and I began a routine of riding over and dropping off tapes for him. He told me I needed a manager and was thinking of who might be good. I told him that he seemed to understand what I was doing so maybe *he* should be my manager. He said he'd think about it.

A few days later he called me and told me he would be my manager and that he'd have a management contract drawn up soon. I was happy. I didn't have anything to manage, but it felt good to at least have someone who knew the record business on my side.

One Saturday morning Carter had a garage sale to clear junk out of his cool Neutra-designed house. I rode my bike over, bought a coffee grinder and a rice steamer, and dropped off my latest tape. Shortly after I rode away, a record producer and friend of Carter's named Davitt Sigerson stopped by the garage sale. While he was there, Carter handed Davitt the tape I had just left and said, "Check this kid out."

Davitt listened to the tape in his car and called Carter when he got home. He told Carter that he liked the tape a lot and wanted to produce me. Carter arranged for Davitt and me to meet for breakfast at a restaurant on Santa Monica Boulevard a few days later. As we had breakfast, I sat across from the bearded and bespectacled denim-clad producer and told him of my intentions: I had a lot of musical ideas in me and I wanted to grow and evolve, trying different things over the years. He said he thought I was going to get the chance to do that.

This was exciting. After years of solid rejection, a real record producer was seriously interested in me. I still didn't have a recording contract, but I had another person on my side who was passionate about my music. I had been sinking into the deepest depression yet, living above a garage in late 1980s Los Angeles, but now I had at least *some* hope.

Soon after my meeting with Davitt, out of the blue—Davitt was offered the job of being *president* of Polydor Records. This was pretty amazing since he had previously been a recording artist himself, then a record producer, but had never worked for a record company. He took the job and called Carter to tell him that he was now unable to produce me but, as president of Polydor Records, he wanted one of his first signings to be . . . me.

Carter called me at the magazine office to tell me the news. He said it would be a very small deal to make two albums for Polydor. I hung up the phone and walked down the hall, feeling lighter than air. This was the greatest, most amazing day. It was, indeed, a very small deal, but I didn't care. All I heard was "make two albums." That was enough for me. The deal paid just enough so I could quit the job I had been at for two years now, and hated, and devote all my time to writing and recording and still squeak by. Washing out the boss's coffee mug was something I almost relished during my last two weeks on the job, knowing it would be over soon.

You see, it's things like this that make it hard for me to

let the darker moments in my life beat me down too much. When something like this is possible, and actually happens, how can I be so cynical? I was a clueless kid who left his mom's house in Virginia to see if he could do something with his music on the opposite side of the country, with absolutely no idea what the possibilities were or what I was getting into. And *something was happening*. I was now able to be one of those rare, lucky people who gets to do what they want and have to do—and get paid for it, even.

The second greatest day of my life was going up the elevator of the PolyGram building to my first meeting at Polydor. I was actually being asked to a meeting about *my* upcoming album in the building I had revered from across the street with a hose in my hand.

I began to meet with music publishers who were interested in publishing my songs. One of them, Betsy Anthony, introduced me to one of her songwriters named Parthenon Huxley. He had half a beard, different-color shoes, and one side of his head had long hair while the other side had short hair. He invited me to his weird little house on the steepest hill in Echo Park. I had never been around any artistically minded people and this was all fascinating to me. I loved hanging out at his house and being around people that weren't only interested in pickup trucks and tractor pulls. Echo Park was full of all sorts of artists.

Soon I moved to a little house on a scary alley in Echo Park. My car window was repeatedly smashed and the stereo was always being stolen, but it was worth it to be in this new world. I began dating the sister of Parthenon's wife— my first girlfriend in years. I asked Parthenon if he wanted to produce my record with me and we got to work at his neighbor Jim Lang's tiny home-studio, directly across the street from Parthenon's house. Everything was going nicely.

I didn't have any real vision for production and was just happy to be making a record. This was 1991, which was basically still the late 1980s, and the production values were not so great, to say the least. If I hear any of the record we made now, I cringe at the cheesy reverb and instrumentation of some of the tracks. But it wasn't without its oddball charm, I suppose.

We finished the record quickly, all made on an extremely low budget, and were told it would come out in February of the coming year, 1992.

Meanwhile, my mom called to tell me that my dog Fido, who was now thirteen, was having severe leg trouble and needed to be "put to sleep." (I love that term . . . I guess it's too hard to say that it was time to kill my dog.) Ma wasn't up to it, so I flew back to Virginia to take care of the grisly deed. I was very businesslike about the whole affair, but then, when the vet actually gave the shot, watching Fido's tail wag a few last wags was devastating, and I had to lock myself in the bathroom where I sobbed uncontrollably like a baby.

Liz was now living with Virginia's biggest drug dealer

kingpin, who had just been released from prison, and my mom now had a boyfriend, Bill, who was much older than my mom—in his eighties. He was so old he knew one of the Wright brothers—the guys who invented *FLIGHT*. While I was sitting in my mom's dining room reading the paper one morning, I overheard this conversation between my mom and Bill:

Mom: "Let's go down to Kitty Hawk some weekend."

Bill: "Kitty Hawk?"

Mom: "Yeah. Kitty Hawk. You know, where the Wright brothers are from."

Bill: "The Wright Brothers? Oh, yeah! I used to know Orville."

A MAN CALLED E CAME OUT AS SCHEDULED. AS usual, I had no idea what to expect. One morning I was sitting in my Echo Park kitchen, turning the dial on the radio, when I heard the sounds of the album's appropriately titled first song, "Hello Cruel World," being played on KROQ, the "alternative" rock station, *my* voice singing:

> *Norman Rockwell colors fade*
> *All my favorite things have changed*
> *But what the hell*
> *Hello cruel world*

Holy shit! I was on the radio. I called my girlfriend and yelled, "I'm on the radio!" and put the phone up to the radio, just like they do in the movies when someone hears themselves on the radio for the first time. As the last note of the song trailed off, the disc jockey announced: "That was EEEEE . . . Sounds like a hit to me!"

The song actually did become an alternative rock (whatever that means) hit. It was on the radio all the time and the record company wanted me to go on tour. I didn't realize how unusual it was that I had been signed to a record deal, put out a record, had a hit, and all without ever performing live once. I hadn't been in front of an audience since I was a drummer back in Virginia.

There was a lot of trepidation at the record company about how I would be as a stage performer. No one had high expectations for the kid who records in his closet. Everyone, including myself, was surprised to discover that I had a thing for playing live. When they sent me out across the country as the opening act for Tori Amos's first American tour, I had never performed as a front man anywhere in my life. I'd only been behind the drums at parties and bars in Virginia. And being an opening act is usually a thankless task, I'd heard, but the audiences were really responding, even asking me back for encores.

After the tour, Parthenon and his wife moved into a house at the top of the hill and I moved into Parthenon's weird little house halfway up the hill. Then my girlfriend broke up with me. She was a fascinating, artistic person who was a great writer and it was all such an exciting world for me to be in—we even survived the LA riots together—but she put me through a real roller-coaster ride that we both have come to refer to since as my "Vietnam" (more on this next chapter). I was crushed and began to write lots of songs obsessing on the breakup, which I then recorded for my second Polydor album, called *Broken Toy Shop*. It had lots of songs about how miserable I was and how much I hated her new boyfriend. Songs like "She Loves a Puppet":

> *Got no soul*
> *Only a haircut*
> *He's no man*
> *Barely a boy*
> *Why can't she understand*
> *That I am her true love*
>
> *She loves a puppet*

Broken Toy Shop came out in December 1993, just as there was a big shake-up at PolyGram. Carter called one night to tell me that Davitt would no longer be at Polydor and that the new record didn't have a chance of being noticed or heard now. I asked him what happens next and, in his usual blunt way, he said: "Oh, you'll be dropped."

9

I LOVE CRAZY GIRLS

OK, THIS IS A TOUCHY SUBJECT, AND NOT ONE I'm really comfortable discussing—because I know that it ultimately means that I've been a crazy boy. But right about now in the story, having met my first girlfriend in years, embarking on a hellish tour of duty and subsequently breaking up, it seems like a good time to address the issue. Let's look at the history.

Historically speaking, if I was in a room and there was someone in that room who could make my life an utter hell on earth, I would find that person, hope they would engage me in conversation, feel like I'd found the lost piece to my puzzle, see pictures in my head of us waking up together, our children, our adjoining burial plots fifty years down the line, and I'd truly believe that it was all for the best. For some reason, God made the women I'm attracted to crazy. But since I don't believe in God, then I guess it's just a fact of life that probably has more than a little to do with my upbringing. People I worked with even used to refer to certain kinds of women as "E girls." That's how bad it was.

If she looked like she'd just been sprung from the county mental hospital, I was all over it. I've had a number of girlfriends over the years who could go from hysterical laughter to mournful sobs at the drop of a hat.

Woody Allen had a name for these girls, which he explained in his film *Husbands and Wives*. He called them "Kamikaze women," because they're not just self-destructive, they crash their plane into you, taking you with them.

Let's take the first girlfriend I had, three years after moving to California, my own personal Vietnam experience. I guess it just comes with the dinner, as they say. If you want to be with an interesting, sensitive, artistic type of person, that sensitivity probably means they're going to be sensitive about all sorts of things that you hadn't bargained for. Me and my Vietnam are friends these days, and we can look back on the nightmarish emotional tour of duty with humor all these years later, but it does not, as a waiter might say to the customer ordering a spicy dish that will leave him feeling terrible the next day, "come recommended."

One day she was in love with me, the next day she wasn't sure if she was over her old boyfriend and would go back to him, only to come back to me a day or two later. The roller coaster was speedy and relentless. The boyfriend *before* her old boyfriend called her one night to announce his impending marriage and she called me to come console her, even though she had told me she couldn't see me any more the day before (I, of course, went and consoled her). For her birthday, I wrote a pretty song called "Manchester Girl" for her, thinking it was the most beautiful, real thing I could give her. She hated it. Said that the line about "Pandora's litter box" made her sound like a bad housekeeper. Still, when she dumped me, I was devastated!

Then there was the girlfriend who randomly took her shirt off in the car on our first date, displaying her breasts while I was driving to the restaurant for dinner. After dinner we came home, sat on the couch, and started to kiss. As we were kissing, she started crying and ran to her car and drove off. She called me the next night and explained that she ran off because she had felt the presence of her former boyfriend in the room.

Yet I continued to see her. Another night she called me, ready to kill herself because she had heard that her ex had a new girlfriend. I spent the night talking her down.

Then there was the one who was always jealous over

imaginary liaisons that I was never having, who slammed the bedroom door so hard during one psychotic fit that a mirror fell off a wall and smashed all over the floor. I'm sure the neighbors enjoyed that one, and thanks for the seven years of bad luck (it worked).

Or what about the one who, while lying in bed one night, snapped the immortal line:

"IS WATCHING DAVID FUCKING LETTERMAN MORE IMPORTANT THAN SPOONING ME?"

The list goes on and on.

Maybe this sounds like my life is a little more exciting than it actually is. Keep in mind that these examples are spread over a long period of time, about twenty years actually, with plenty of "dry spells" and not-so-crazy times in between.

Now, when I say crazy, I want you to know that I did draw the line at a certain point. I'm not talking about full-on schizophrenic-type crazy. That's too much, even for me. But some of these were getting close at times.

What is it that attracted me to these lost lambs? Probably a combination of things, not least of which being that I was a lost lamb myself, so I probably felt safe with them (ironic, I know). Growing up in a crazy family sets you up for this kind of thing, if you're not careful. And maybe I was willing to ride along through the roller coaster's low valleys in the name of the oh so glorious peaks. But, as the years went on, the appeal of the crazies has lessened, from sheer exhaustion.

They haven't *all* been crazy, but I have to face up to the fact that, more often than not, they have been. I suppose we're all crazy, really. Some of us just find different ways to deal with it. Look at me and my sister. We are two sides of the same coin. We just dealt with our troubles in different ways: she felt no sense of self and dove into a drug- and alcohol-clouded spiral. I threw myself into my songs. I just got lucky that my method was more constructive.

Also, in their defense, I'm not the easiest person in the world to live with. In some ways I am, once you accept that I'm always working on something, and if I'm not, I tend to keep to myself a lot while I'm cooking up ideas in my head. You have to be a very secure person to be with someone like that, so I've probably been going about this all wrong all these years, trying to make a bad match.

I have great love for each and every one of my crazy girls and don't regret the experiences with any of them (well, most of them. Some of them were *really* bad).

To all the crazy girls I've loved before: thank you, but I'm just too tired now.

10

A DAY AT THE BEACH/ HONOLULU HURRICANE

I WALKED OUT OF THE HOUSE ONE MORNING and had no idea where to go. I got in my little white pickup truck and started driving with no direction in mind. I ended up at Zuma Beach, an hour away from Echo Park. I don't know why I ended up there, something seemed to take me there instinctively. Maybe it was the Neil Young *Zuma* album Liz and I used to play a lot. It was a windy and gray, cloudy weekday morning. The beach was deserted. I got out of the truck and walked out onto the sand and stared at the breaking waves. The only thing I could feel was the urge to walk into them and keep walking until I was underwater.

I finally had a purpose in my life and it was being taken away. I could still make my tapes like always, but I wasn't going to be able to have people hear them now and I wouldn't be able to devote all my time to them. The greatest thing that had ever happened to me was over, so quickly. My plan for all the musical things I wanted to do had just gotten started. I didn't know what to do with myself.

I walked closer and stood right at the point where the tide meets the dry sand. I could feel the springs in my heels about to push me toward the water. I stood there for what felt like a long time, but was probably only ten minutes.

I decided I was too chicken to walk into the ocean. I don't like cold water. I drove back to my little house on the steep hill and laid down on my bed and cried.

Carter booked a short tour of California where I would show up at some bars and play by myself. I practiced for weeks in my basement and bought a shell for the back of my truck to load my gear into. No one came to any of the shows except the one in San Luis Obispo, only because it happened to be full of frat boys who were there anyway, on a night where I was almost beat up twice. Once as I was walking to the bar, when a group of frat boy dickheads randomly circled me on the sidewalk and yelled drunken nonsense at me, and once during my "show" when an inebriated idiot was yelling at me and I made the mistake of yelling back. As I drove my truck along the Pacific Coast

Highway through Big Sur on my way to San Francisco later that night, I had to keep fighting the urge to take a left off the cliff and into the ocean.

I pressed on writing and recording songs in my cold, tiny basement. I didn't know what else to do. I now had eight tracks to work with and some better instruments, at least. I just kept going, blindly.

You often hear actors and film people talking about their work, saying things like, "it was an interesting choice to make, as an actor . . ." I've always been fascinated by this concept of making choices in your work, because I don't think in terms of choices. I only feel what is there that is coming out, and it must be real, so there it is. I don't feel like I have choices. I just do it. It's not so great. Sometimes you feel like there's a gun to your head.

When I was a teenager, I used to make these really weird sound collages on my two-track reel-to-reel machine and send them to Liz in Hawaii. She must have thought I was out of my mind, because these tapes were really out there. Classical records mixed with weird voices I was doing, bursts of rock music, little skits . . . really crazy stuff.

Liz called me and mentioned that she had just come across one of those old tapes I'd sent her. When I got off the phone I thought about how much fun it was making those weird sound collages. Then one day during this bleak period of my life, I was driving down the road and heard the English group Portishead on the radio for the first time and it stopped me cold. I had to pull the truck over to the side of the road so I could really listen. The combination of "loops" made from drum patterns mixed with old Lalo Schifrin film-score samples and the singer's voice on top of it all fascinated me, and I was immediately inspired to get back into my old sound-collage world—but apply it to my new songwriting world.

The new technology had given the world of sound collage so many new possibilities. I called friends and asked if they had any friends who did music on computers and got a few phone numbers. It was an exciting new world that meant all sorts of limitless possibilities in my mind. I felt artistically rejuvenated. One of the first songs I did around this time was called "Novocaine for the Soul." I had written the phrase on a scrap of paper some time earlier, and put it in my pocket with another scrap that I had written the words "Before I sputter out" on and another that said "Jesus and his lawyer are coming back." They were little ideas I was coming up with for a song I wanted to write about how desperate I'd been feeling.

Jennifer Condos, a bass player and friend I had worked with, told me that her husband, Mark Goldenberg, had a computer. I went over to their house and Mark and I made some drum loops and then I went home and came up with a guitar part, lyrics, melody, and then put everything else on top of it on my eight-track in one night. I took the tape back over to Mark's so he could play the guitar solo.

(Jennifer replaced my keyboard bass part with bass guitar, but has never been credited for it due to a clerical error— sorry, Jen! I know it's kind of late.)

> *Life is white*
> *And I am black*
> *Jesus and his lawyer*
> *Are coming back*
> *Oh my darling*
> *Will you be here*
> *Before I sputter out*

I was excited about the song. It felt like I was getting into something really different. Parthenon gave me the number of a guy he'd worked with, Jim Jacobsen, who did stuff on his computer as well. I made a song called "Susan's House" partially at his house and partially in my basement, in a similar working fashion to the "Novocaine" recording process. That one was even more of a departure from the stuff I had been doing—I was speaking most of the vocal part instead of singing it. I wanted to get outside of my head for a song and take a walk through the neighborhood. I thought, Who says I have to *sing*?

> *Going over to Susan's house*
> *Walking south down Baxter Street*
> *Nothing hiding behind this picket fence*

There's a crazy old woman smashing bottles
Where her house burned down two years ago
People say that back then she really wasn't that
      crazy

Then a piano sample from an old Gladys Knight record I had plays, intermingling with a bunch of sound effects and the beat of my walk through the neighborhood. I had met the Susan the song was named after a couple of years earlier, but we had already broken up by the time I was writing the song and, in truth, her house was in Pasadena, much too far to walk to. Sometimes you have to take a little artistic license in the name of getting to some universal truth, or whatever you call it. For the record, Susan was not a crazy girl (a rare exception at this point in my life) and had to suffer through meeting me just as I was releasing an album about how heartbroken I was over my last girlfriend (Vietnam).

I did songs called "Flower" and "Your Lucky Day in Hell" with these guys, in the same working manner. All of these were done the first time we tried them and never changed again during the years before their release on record.

Meanwhile, I did about seventy more songs on my own in my basement. Being interested in sampling woke me up and I found myself interested in modern music for the first time since Prince popped into my life. I also liked the Japanese group Pizzicato Five, and Nirvana, Hole, and Liz

Phair were making new records that felt honest and real to me. It felt like the stuff I was writing now was more immediate and vibrant than the stuff I had been doing before. I was trying to strip away some layers and get more to the reality underneath everything. I started to learn more and develop ideas about production. I stopped using cheesy reverb so much. I felt like I'd been hiding and now I wanted to be very upfront and dry, even if it made me uncomfortable. Just like this book.

One of the songs I recorded came about when my friend Jon Brion came over to my house one night. He was a child prodigy who grew into a man who could play any instrument extremely well, and could accompany anyone, on the spot, without rehearsing or anything, and he had tons of amazing old instruments and recording equipment. He came over and suggested, as an exercise, that he would go upstairs for thirty minutes to write a song while I went downstairs for thirty minutes to write a song. He was always coming up with ideas like this. "Write a song about something on this table . . ." and so forth. I went downstairs, picked up my paisley Telecaster guitar, plugged it into the tape recorder, and started singing:

My beloved monster and me
We go everywhere together
Wearin' a raincoat that has four sleeves
Gets us through all kinds of weather

I recorded the guitar and vocal right there and, when the thirty minutes was up, invited Jon down to hear what I'd done. He liked it and said we should take what I recorded over to his studio in Silver Lake soon and add other instruments, which we did a few days later. Jon added trombone, bass, a bunch of keyboards, and the sound of a credit card brushing over his beard stubble to my guitar and vocal part. We both banged tool kits, and any metal we could find, up and down on the floor for percussion.

Carter was now working as an A&R man again, at the PolyGram empire that had left me behind. There was no place for me there but he was still willing to manage me, although there was nothing to manage now. He liked the stuff I was doing and suggested I start working under a different name, since I seemed to have made a big leap, musically. He said he even had the name for me, "EELS." I liked the idea of working under a different name. I'd had a lot of logistical problems being billed simply as E. If you see "APPEARING TONIGHT: E" in the paper, you might not even notice the E. I needed a few more letters and Carter thought having the new name start with an E would mean my previous CDs could still be near my new CDs in the record stores. (It wasn't until the first EELS CD finally came out that I was in a record store and saw that there were countless Eagles and Earth, Wind, and Fire CDs keeping my old and new CDs apart from each other. Must think these things through more.)

Carter started playing some of my new tapes to record companies, but there wasn't much interest. He was playing them "Novocaine for the Soul," "Susan's House," etc., exactly as they are on the album that came out years later.

One night I was walking down the Third Street Promenade in Santa Monica and heard someone say, "Hey, E!" A blond-haired guy who looked vaguely familiar approached me. It was Chris Douridas, the program director from the local public radio station, KCRW. I had performed on his show a couple of times when the E albums came out. He asked what I had been up to and I told him I had been recording new stuff. He asked if he could hear some of it and I said I'd send him a tape. I figured he was just being polite and making conversation, but I sent a tape to KCRW the next day, just in case.

A few mornings later I got a call from an assistant at KCRW saying that Chris was trying to play my tape on the air, but it was malfunctioning and he wanted to know if I could bring over a better copy. I got in my truck and drove across town to hand-deliver a better-working tape. Chris wanted to play "Novocaine for the Soul." While I was still standing there, he tested my new tape and then played it on the air.

Carter encouraged me to put a live act together to play these new songs. That was a real challenge, as these were very studio-influenced recordings. And some of my other new songs were very electric guitar–centered, another new thing for me. So I set out to form a live group that could hopefully do both: rock the house and be versatile enough to rise to the challenge of some of the more complicated, studio-centric songs.

Jonathan Norton had played drums with me a little for what was going to be the tour for my second album, but the tour never happened when the shake-up at PolyGram occurred. He was a big guy with a long ponytail and a penchant for African djembe drums and world percussion. He looked like a roadie for the Grateful Dead. He heard that I was forming something to play new stuff and lobbied hard for the drummer job. I told him I didn't think he was the right guy. Too world music–oriented, too "ponytail."

Sometime later he came over to my house and I barely recognized him. He had cut off his ponytail, grown a beard, and dyed his hair blond. He was trying to tell me that he wasn't just those things I thought he was, and he was showing me how badly he wanted to play with me. I was impressed that he had gone this far, and I didn't have anyone better in mind, so I agreed to give him a try. I went out to his garage in Northridge and plugged my Les Paul guitar into my little Fender amp and started playing the arpeggiated chords to "Novocaine for the Soul" with lots of tremolo and distortion, different than the sound of the recording. Jonathan started thumping his hands on his drums. I had never been the electric guitarist in a band before and it was exciting and scary to have this new responsibility. Something was clicking and we both knew it. This was going to be something I could actually do in a live setting. I didn't care if it didn't sound like the recording. I liked that it sounded different. They both sounded good to me, in different ways, and I realized that there was no reason to treat a recording and a live performance the same way. They were totally different situations.

I needed a bass player and a keyboardist now. We tried a couple of bass players and agreed that the best choice seemed to be Tommy Walter, a guy I knew from a local band called Mrs. God. He was a good player and could also play the French horn. One day we were playing in the garage and I commented that Jonathan needed a good nickname. Tommy said, "Yeah, like 'Butch,'" and Jonathan liked it to the point of referring to himself in the third person as "Butch" often, so it stuck.

We had trouble finding a suitable keyboardist that could handle all the samples involved in some of the songs. We only had one choice, and I can't remember his name now, but he was a really flaky guy who didn't show up on what was to be his first day. He left a long, rambling phone message later about how he got stuck in traffic and then got lost and then . . . we cut up his message and made a sound collage out of it for our amusement. I decided to go without a keyboardist and not have any samples when playing live. I figured we were sounding really strong as a three-piece and I could play a keyboard myself sometimes.

I had borrowed an old Hohner Cembalet keyboard that I liked a lot from Jon Brion. It was like a little electric piano, the size of an electric guitar case, like something the girl in the Archie comics would play, and one day I decided to plug it into my guitar amp to see what that would sound like. I loved the sound. It was like a cross between a piano and an electric guitar that I had never heard before. But the keys weren't dynamic, meaning that when you touched a key it was always the same volume. I needed something more sensitive to the dynamics of my songs—sometimes I needed to rock, other times I needed to play something quiet and pretty—so I asked Jon for advice and he told me that an old Wurlitzer electric piano would be the closest thing to the Cembalet sound, but with touch-sensitive keys. I opened the want ads and found one in great shape, cheap. No one cared about Wurlitzer pianos anymore, the sound was considered old and cheesy.

We played our first show at a tiny coffeehouse on Melrose Avenue called Beetlejuice. I asked my friend Aimee Mann to introduce us, and to just say something like, "Ladies and gentlemen, the EELS!" but she said, "Ladies and gentlemen, here's E with some side guys." (Never ask Aimee Mann to introduce your band for the first time.) It was apparent right from the start, when we crashed into "Novocaine for the Soul," that something was happening here and I did know what it was, Mr. Jones. It felt like we were going to explode through the walls of the tiny coffeehouse.

Aimee came up to me after the set and said, "Wow. What the fuck was that?" Everyone seemed really excited about it. KCRW was playing my tapes and a "buzz" started to go around town. This was all completely new to me and quite unlike my first go-around with the music business.

Eventually several record companies were interested in my new thing. All the attention, after my day at Zuma Beach, was exciting, but surreal and hard to soak in. Elton John had heard my tape and I got word that he was interested in possibly signing me to his record label. He invited us to the Hollywood Bowl to meet with him and watch his concert. Butch chewed Elton's ear off backstage. Every step is mapped out in advance for Elton at his concerts, but something went wrong and we accidentally ran into him in the long corridor beneath the Hollywood Bowl as we were being escorted to a holding tank where he was supposed to greet us later.

Butch: "Hey, Elton!"

Elton nervously looks at his security guards. Then says, "Uh . . . Hello."

Butch: "How's it going, Elton?"

Elton, growing more disoriented and unsure of what to do, says, "I'm well, thank you."

Butch: "So where you goin' after this, Elton?"

Elton says, "Home to Atlanta," and then does some kind of ear pulling/eye winking gesture so his entourage will usher him down the hallway, which they do.

We get ushered into the holding tank but don't see Elton again that evening. We never heard from him again, actually, but there were still several record labels all wanting to put out my new records.

It was getting weirder and weirder. Suddenly I was being offered obscene amounts of money to do what I loved. This wasn't like my previous modest experience at all. I was being wined and dined by record executives from almost every label. A&R men would come out to the garage and play croquet with us, bring us pizza, do anything to pal around with us. It was crazy. If I told you how much money I was being offered, you wouldn't believe it. It was well beyond anything I could have dreamed. The label offering the most money was Interscope Records. Everyone around me said to go with whoever offers the most money.

But I had respect for Lenny Waronker and Mo Ostin, who were just starting up the new DreamWorks Records label. They were well known for being the artist-friendly record executives during Warner Brothers Records' artistic heyday, and Lenny had even produced Randy Newman's *Good Old Boys* album, one of my old favorites. Having left Warner Brothers when they lost their autonomy during a corporate shake-up, they were just starting up this new label and hadn't put out any records yet. They were offering less money than Interscope, but it was still a huge amount compared to my first deal, so whatever. I was now out of money and was about to have to get a job. My accountant was going to drop me, tired of making a percentage of nothing. But it looked like that was all going to be solved now, no matter who I went with, although it could all be over very soon, as I had already learned. I went against the advice of everyone around me and signed with Lenny and Mo, to be the first band on the new label.

It was the smartest decision I ever made. The biggest money offer would've expected the biggest money return, not the best music I could make to my ability. After one record, I would have been back washing cars across from the PolyGram building. (Several years later Interscope bought DreamWorks Records and I ended up becoming part of their empire anyway, so, uh, all is forgiven, right? Right?)

DreamWorks started to put together an impressive roster of interesting artists. Shortly after I signed on, I was happy to hear that Lenny intended to bring in Elliott Smith, a singer and friend of ours who we all admired a lot, as his next signing to the label. It felt like a nice place to be with such great company on the roster.

Being the subject of an aggressive bidding war was so dizzying and stressful, I had to spend a week locked up alone in a cabin in Big Sur after it was over, just to decompress and gather my wits. I felt like I'd been through some kind of battle where everyone was losing their minds.

When I got back I put together a list of twelve or thirteen tracks from my seventy-something songs to make up the first EELS album. Most of them were finished the day I recorded them and would go on the record exactly as I'd left them, no remixing or anything. But there were a few of the electric guitar songs that I thought could be better if I recorded them with the new live band, so we set up in a little garage in Burbank with Mike Simpson of the Dust Brothers, who had produced The Beastie Boys' *Paul's Boutique* and Tone Loc's *Wild Thing*, to record three or four songs with Butch and Tommy, so they could at least make some appearance on the album.

I called the album *Beautiful Freak* after a song that was inspired by Susan.

You're such a beautiful freak
I wish there were more just like you
You're not like all of the others
And that is why I love you
Beautiful freak

Perhaps if I hadn't referred to her as a "freak" she'd still be my girlfriend.

I wanted to have a photo of a little girl with big eyes on the album cover. At the photo session, I was surprised to see that the little girl who came in to have her photo taken looked like a miniature Susan. An odd coincidence.

With twelve of my seventy-some songs on it, we had the album mastered and the advance copies were pressed up and sent out to all the radio stations and the press. My mom and Liz were excited about my second chance. Liz was always bragging about me to her friends and playing my music for anyone who would or wouldn't listen.

One night just before the album's release, we played a show at the Alligator Lounge, a dingy little club next to the 10 freeway that we played at a lot. I came home after the show and checked my phone messages. I threw my keys on the kitchen table and pressed play on the answering machine. There was a message from my mom, who sounded really weird, saying to call her. Then there was another message from her, "Liz took a bottle of pills and . . . she went into a coma. Um . . . call . . . me."

I quickly dialed my mom's number. She answered, her voice shaky.

"What happened?" I asked.

"She took a bottle of pills and went into a coma . . . and she . . . she . . . she . . ."

There was a long pause. Then, "She died."

When I heard those two words, it felt like someone punched me in the stomach. The kitchen started spinning around me. Tears filled my eyes. I yelled into the receiver, "NO!" My mom was sobbing on the other end.

Liz had tried to kill herself several times since that first time we found her on the bathroom floor back in The Summer of Love, but hearing that she actually had succeeded and was no longer alive was too much to fathom. When I got off the phone, I fell on the hallway floor and sobbed uncontrollably, moaning her name over and over.

She had been getting even worse and had been leaving me phone messages that were increasingly bizarre and nonsensical. She had married her drug kingpin boyfriend while he was in prison. When he got out, they lived in Virginia briefly and then moved to Hawaii. Even after her first sour Hawaiian getaway, she was willing to try it again. She was in and out of mental hospitals and drug rehabs constantly. Then she wrote a note about going to join our father in a parallel universe, swallowed a bottle of pills, and killed herself for real this time.

She just wasn't equipped to survive in this world. Between the strain of family madness she inherited and the crazy way we were brought up, she had no sense of self or sanity in her world. She tried to fill the bottomless pit inside her heart with every drug she could get her hands on, but nothing helped.

She was my biggest fan. She was always really supportive of my music and asking me to send her more. From my weird old sound collages to my latest new stuff, I always sent it to her as soon as it was ready. I had just mailed her an advance copy of *Beautiful Freak*, eager for her reaction to the mix of the old collage tapes I made for her with my newer songwriting, but I don't think she got it before she died.

I was in the midst of the most unexpected and exciting time of my life, but now all I could think about was Liz. The juxtaposition of such extreme highs and lows happening simultaneously was really hard to handle and just plain weird. I told my mom that I would pay for the funeral but to keep it a secret from Liz's husband. I didn't want him to know that I had any money. I flew to Honolulu and met my mom, who flew in from Virginia, at a Holiday Inn by the airport, where we both stayed for the week.

The night before Liz's body was to be cremated, the funeral parlor held an open-casket viewing of her body, so her friends and family could say goodbye. My mom and I got there early and walked up to the coffin. The funeral director opened the lid and I couldn't recognize the person lying there. They did a ghastly makeup job on her. Liz didn't wear makeup that much and this looked like another person, with very heavy makeup, and quite a scary person at that. My mom seemed oblivious to this and started snapping photos of her.

They put on a tape of cheesy funeral organ music and one of Liz's crazy friends from the mental hospital came in and approached the coffin. She looked at Liz's face and shrieked in horror, causing the other attendees to all look over in unison, startled. I rolled my eyes, sighed, and ran over to give Liz the last gift I could give her. I closed the lid of her coffin.

After a while I couldn't take any more, so I snuck out and went to the nearest place, Fuddruckers, a TGI Fridays–like chain restaurant across the street, for a beer and something to eat. I was in a daze and just needed to do something that didn't involve my sister dying or a funeral parlor for a half-hour or so. I sat there, ignored, for twenty minutes and finally got up and asked a manager if someone could take my order. Finally I got to order. Another thirty minutes later, my sandwich and beer showed up. I bit into the sandwich, which was smothered in mayonnaise, which I had asked them to leave off. I hate mayonnaise. This wasn't the day to put mayonnaise on my sandwich. I drank the beer, hoping it would numb me a little from the hell I was in and paid the check. As I was walking out, I noticed a guest book at the front counter. I picked up the pen tied to the book and wrote "THIS PLACE SUCKS." As I finished writing the word SUCKS, the manager came up behind me, looked at what I had written, and asked me to leave the premises.

I walked across the street, thinking how it wouldn't be so bad if one of the cars hit me, and snuck back in the back door of the funeral parlor, where a couple of Liz's friends, her husband, and my mom were milling about. Every moment was excruciating.

The next day there was a small ceremony on a hill overlooking the ocean where we all laid palm leaves on a small box containing Liz's ashes. It was a beautiful, breezy, and sunny Hawaiian day. The sky and ocean were deep blue. I hid behind my sunglasses thinking about Liz, wanting it to end. On the way there my mother and I were arguing in the car about how to get there and now she was smiling, like it wasn't a big deal that she was at her daughter's funeral. I clenched my teeth, seething with anger over the idea that Liz was raised by a woman who was always caring for her in the physical world, but really was, essentially, just a little girl emotionally. I grew increasingly frustrated with my mom's indecisiveness and the lonely feeling that I was the only adult involved in all of this.

Afterward, my mom and I went back to the hotel and back to our separate rooms. She was flying back to Virginia in the morning and I was flying back to Los Angeles, where I had a show to play with the band. As I sat in my room I grew even sadder, thinking about what it must be like for my mother, sitting in her shitty airport hotel room, having just returned from the funeral of her only daughter, who she never stopped taking care of.

11

HAPPY TRAILS

"I'M GETTING TIRED OF HEARING THAT BLOKE
sing about your fucking house every twenty minutes."

An English friend of Susan's had written her a postcard,
knowing that she was the Susan who lived in the house I
was singing about on the radio. The *Beautiful Freak* album
was finally released in August of 1996 and "Novocaine for
the Soul" and "Susan's House" were being played on ra-
dios around the world.

The day after I returned from Honolulu to Echo Park,
my landlady, Francis, an eighty-something-year-old
woman from Missouri who lived next door to me, knocked
on my door.

"Hi, E," she said in her wobbly Midwest rasp. "How was your trip?"

"It was nice."

I hadn't told her that I was there because my sister had committed suicide. I didn't want to get into it. Francis put her hand on the porch railing to steady her bulky frame.

"Listen, E, I don't know if you know this, but I can see apparitions."

"What?"

"I can see apparitions."

I looked at her.

"Ghosts."

"Really?"

"Yes. And I thought I should tell you something. Before you got back yesterday, I saw a young woman walk into your house."

"You did?"

"Yes, I did."

Initially, it really spooked me when Francis told me this, and I was feeling a little scared about sleeping in the house that night. But then I thought about the timing of it and tried to look at it in a more positive, less spooky, light. Kooky or not, I liked the idea of Liz coming by to say goodbye one last time, even if she just missed me by a few hours. If there's gonna be a ghost in your house, you might as well think of it as a friendly ghost.

One morning soon after, I was making tea when I heard

what sounded like a bunch of kittens meowing from under the floor of my kitchen. I put my ear to the floor and it became clear that there was definitely something alive under there. I called Parthenon's wife, Janet, who was the neighborhood cat lady and a good friend of mine. She was always taking care of ten to twenty stray cats at any given time. She was an expert and I didn't have a clue what to do.

Janet came over and we went down to my little studio in the basement, moved the filing cabinet out of the closet, and opened the trapdoor that went to the crawl space under the kitchen. The sound of kittens got louder as I crawled on the dirt floor in the dark. They seemed to be inside a little cubbyhole enclosed by walls on all sides except the top. With great trepidation I reached my arm up and over, into the black hole, afraid of what might happen. I felt something furry, grabbed it, and brought it out. It was a tiny, black kitten. I handed the kitten to Janet and she put it in a little cardboard box she'd brought. I kept dipping my arm back in until I had handed Janet three more black kittens.

Janet set up a large cage on my porch that we put the four kittens in. As we were putting the kittens in the cage, the mother, a skittish, scrawny stray, suddenly appeared on the porch and approached us cautiously. Janet was very gentle and warm to the mother (she was kind of a cat whisperer, if you will). She instructed me on how to give some medicine to the kittens with a dropper. The mother watched as I held one of the kittens in my palm and fed him the medicine with the dropper. Then the mother ran away, toward the empty lot down the hill on the other side of my house.

A few minutes later the mother came back with a fifth kitten in her mouth, approached me, and set the kitten on the ground in front of me. This is still one of the cutest things I've ever seen, like something from a Wonderful World of Disney movie when I was a kid. Then the mother ran away again to the empty lot next door and returned with a sixth kitten in her mouth, which she also presented to me. I named the mother "Slinky" and tried not to get too attached to the kittens, since I was allergic to cats. I found homes for all of the kittens, but most of them turned out to be pretty shitty house pets. Too much stray, wild blood in them. But I got attached to Slinky and kept her around.

I left my landlady, Francis, in charge of feeding Slinky while I left Echo Park to tour the world. I flew to our first stop, opening for the band Lush in Indianapolis, where I was met at the airport by a guy named "Spider," who was going to be our roadie. Aimee Mann had recommended him, but it didn't feel like a good fit to me. He had a ton of earrings dangling from his ear, spoke loudly in a thick Boston accent, and occasionally dropped references to his time in prison, which scared us all. But as the tour went on, it became clear that Spider was a dedicated worker and friend who we'd even go so far as have perform as our opening act at some of our shows, playing his own songs.

"Novocaine for the Soul" became a number one "alternative" radio hit. I had little time to notice this, as I was always riding somewhere to get to a sound check or interview and never seemed to have enough time to do the little things we all take for granted, like sleep. We quickly graduated from opening for bands to doing our own shows. I was seeing parts of the world I never thought I'd see. It was all very exciting but surreal and sad at the same time, having just returned from Liz's funeral.

It's all a blur of airports, vans, tour buses, TV studios, and concerts to me now. Although it was exciting, I started to get an uneasy gut feeling about the whole experience. I noticed that everyone around me seemed to be focused on selling records more than anything else. It was nice that the record company was excited—a real change from my previous experience. But every time I heard one of the musicians in the band refer to a town we were going to as a "market," my stomach ached.

I didn't write the song "Beautiful Freak" about a car. I wrote it about someone who is truly different, not fashionably different or "edgy" as the advertising executives love to say. Nevertheless, Volkswagen wanted to use it for a commercial. I couldn't even consider it. The so-called alternative culture brought with it an ugly new reality: it wasn't really an alternative at all. It was for sale just like anything else in the mall. It was rebelling against nothing. It just looked like a rebel and made the motions and noises of a rebel, but it wasn't any kind of rebel, or individual, to be sure.

Turning down requests like the Volkswagen ad was starting to get me a "difficult" reputation in the "industry." I was seeing too many people in the audience that I didn't like. We went on the Lollapalooza tour, where a sea of teenage jocks in backwards baseball caps would all give me the finger in unison as we played "Novocaine for the Soul" as a spoken-word piece, complete with bongos and finger snaps, instead of the electric guitar–drum loop-driven song that was booming out of their Jeeps' speakers that summer. One day we were playing when, in between songs, I kept hearing a thin, reedy voice bleating: "I KNOW YOU'RE BATMAN! I KNOW YOU'RE BATMAN!"

I looked down to see Lollapalooza founder Perry Farrell in the front row looking up at me, his fist clutched around the neck of a bottle of red wine. He looked up at me and said it again. "I KNOW YOU'RE BATMAN!"

All these years later, I'm still not sure why I'm Batman. Things were getting really weird. Liz's death happening at the same time as all this gave me a different perspective. I was more aware of a bigger picture, and although I now had what I'd always dreamed of—music was my life—I had to stay on top of it all and think about what I really wanted out of it.

We were getting nominated for MTV awards and all that kind of stuff that people take so seriously, for no apparent reason. In England we won a Brit award and I didn't want to go to any awards shows, so they said they'd send whoever I wanted to present the award to us and film it. I asked for Spinal Tap, a band of actors masquerading as a rock band. The camera crew met us at the record company offices and Spinal Tap's wigs showed up in cases three hours before the actors did. The actors came, put on their wigs, and presented the award to us. They were more real than most of the rock bands out there. We turned the award into a cymbal stand for Butch's drum set so it could function and actually be worth something.

We were in London taping an appearance on *Top of the Pops* when we heard that Princess Diana had died in a car accident. Suddenly our backstage passes with a distorted image of the Princess—big eyes and mushed-up face— weren't so funny. The whole country shut down while the radio played only classical music and "Goodbye England's Rose." There was no way our *Top of the Pops* performance of a song called "Your Lucky Day in Hell" was going to air now. We spent the week sitting around our hotel next door to the Princess's house, Kensington Palace, and watched the masses leave flowers at the gates.

Meanwhile, Liz's death seemed to be making my mom do some soul-searching and she began doing things like saying "I love you" at the end of each phone call, which she never, ever said to Liz or me before. I could tell it was awkward for her and I appreciated the effort. We started to talk like more normal people for the first time. You know, actually talking about something important and emotional. It was weird that all there was left of the family was my mom and me. When we played a show in Washington, D.C., my mom came and watched from the audience. It was fun hanging out with her backstage before and after the show. She seemed excited and proud but also made the occasional critical comment, of course.

Back in Echo Park, Parthenon, Janet, and I had befriended a half-black, half-Cuban kid from the neighborhood named Alan who wanted to become a filmmaker. He always called me "Milkman" but would never tell me why. We pitched in and bought him a video camera for his birthday so he could make funny little films, some of them starring me and Parthenon. It was fun, and it gave me a chance to do something other than worry about the music business or think about Liz. Alan was really poor and his mom was dying from AIDS. We went to visit her in the hospital one day. She was a manic-depressive albino who didn't speak English, and it was obvious that she wasn't long for this earth, as they say. When she died, Alan moved in with Parthenon and Janet. At the funeral I remember watching the forklift lower her particle-board coffin into the ground while I thought about how Alan, who was only fifteen or sixteen, might be feeling. Like he wanted to jump in the hole and pull her back out into his life.

Not long after she died, Alan crashed his friend's car into the wall on my driveway and came running into my house. His personality had completely changed from the sweet-natured kid he had always been. I thought he was on drugs. After shouting all sorts of nonsensical, nasty stuff, he got back in the car and screeched off. He went to the bus station and got on a bus across the country to go see his sister in Florida. In Texas he got thrown off the bus because he wouldn't stop screaming about the aliens he saw on the side of the road. He walked into a video store and trashed it. They arrested him and he spent the night in jail. Walking out of the jailhouse the next day, he came upon an un-attended, but still running, milk truck. He jumped in and took off, starting one of those police chases with helicopters broadcasting it all live on Texas TV. They finally caught him and he went back to jail. Eventually I realized what must be going on. I remembered that his mother was severely bipolar and, knowing that it can be a hereditary disease sometimes, I figured out that he probably wasn't on drugs at all but had just inherited his mother's illness. But he was just a black kid causing trouble to the Texas police and TV audience.

During a short break in touring, I woke up one morning in Echo Park to the sound of sirens at the top of the hill. Janet, my cat whisperer, Parthenon's wife and my ex-girlfriend's sister, was rushed to the hospital after experiencing a metallic taste in her mouth and collapsing. At the hospital, her diagnosis was grim: a grapefruit-sized cancerous brain tumor was growing in her head. It was shocking news. She was so full of life, always busy, doing a million things, laughing . . . and only in her thirties. How could it be?

During this same short break, I was sitting on the porch with Slinky one afternoon when the mail came. There was a letter from my mom that contained a little aside buried in it that said:

By the way, I've had a little cough lately and the doctor is insisting they check it out further, but I'm sure it's nothing to worry about. Just thought I should mention it.

I came through Virginia on tour soon thereafter and went to see my mom. While I was there I told her that I didn't want to be left here all alone, the last one standing, especially so soon. She said not to worry, she wasn't going anywhere.

Janet, who had more energy than anyone I had ever met, was determined to beat the cancer and it seemed like there was a good chance that she would be one of those great survival stories, just because of her sheer tenacity. It was heartbreaking to see it get the best of her. Her long black hair was gone and her face was swollen from the treatments. Her speech became slurred. Eventually she had to be taken to the hospital, where she slipped into a coma. I went to say goodbye, not sure if there was any possibility that she could hear me. Parthenon called me a couple of nights later to tell me that she had died.

A few days later, Janet's sister and I helped Parthenon with the horrible task of packing up Janet's belongings. Before I went over that morning, I went over the hill to pick up some food from Netty's, one of my favorite neighborhood restaurants, so I could bring something for us all to eat before we started packing things up. While I was waiting for the food, I called my mom from the pay phone outside Netty's. She sounded tired. I asked her how she was feeling and she started to hem and haw like she often did, but this was different. This was reminding me of her phone message about Liz.

"Um, well, I have some news."

I braced myself. Nothing good ever starts with "Um, well, I have some news."

"They found a . . ."

A long pause.

"A *what*?" I snapped.

"A . . . (*sigh*) . . . a tumor in my lung."

I felt myself go numb.

"Was it cancerous?" I asked, nervously.

There was another long silence. Before it was over I knew what the silence meant.

"Yes," she finally said.

I was in shock. Standing at the pay phone on Silver Lake Boulevard on Saturday morning, I was about to go help my friend pack up his deceased wife's belongings, and now my mother was telling me she had cancer. The pain of Liz's suicide was still so fresh. This just couldn't be happening.

I asked her, "Well, how bad is it?"

"Um . . . well . . . uh . . ."

"Ma, come on, you have to tell me what the situation is. Are they gonna operate?"

"No. It spread to my lymph nodes . . . and it's too . . . advanced."

The skyline was starting to spin and my legs were getting shaky.

"So . . . so, what's the prognosis then?"

"He says one or two years, maybe, depending on what kind of treatment I do."

This was the moment when I stopped trying to make sense of the world, because this just didn't make sense. How could this happen after Liz had just died?

Later, when I thought about it more, it did make sense in some terrible ways. Besides the fact that my mom was passively breathing in three packs of Kents every day during all those years in the house with my dad, even though the house had been smoke-free for all the years since his death, it also made sense that something like this would develop from the horrible grief that was mostly bottled up inside her after the suicide of her only daughter.

I got the food and drove up the hill to Parthenon's in a daze. When I walked in I saw Janet's suitcase sitting there by the front door, Parthenon having just brought it back from the hospital. The idea of Janet and her suitcase going to the hospital but only her suitcase returning was so sad.

I flew back to Virginia and went to the oncologist with my mom. He explained the different options for her—there weren't many. She could do chemo and radiation, which would be very unpleasant but could probably give her some more time; she could be part of an experimental group for a newer treatment, but would never be able to know if she was getting the actual treatment or the placebo treatment; or she could do nothing. She decided to do chemo and radiation for a while and see how it went.

Through all of this, I had a busy touring schedule: shows that had been booked well in advance, as they have to be. If you don't show up to these shows you could go into financial ruin, owing the money from the concerts back to the promoters. So I was coming and going a lot. My mom was very healthy and active at this point, so I would go off on a leg of a tour, call her every day to make sure she was OK, and come back to Virginia whenever I could. My mom's boyfriend, Bill, if you can call an eighty-five-year-old a "boy," was around, at least. He was a really sweet, gentle man whose wife had left him in the 1950s when she figured out that she was a lesbian. My mom getting sick was a tough blow for him, as he was at least twenty years older than her and she was good at looking after him, more than vice versa.

I bought a dayglo-green punk rock chick wig that I saw in a store window and sent it to my mom. She had already lost most of her hair and was trying out different wigs. She wore the green wig to her chemo appointment one day and the nurses all loved it.

One evening I flew back in to Dulles Airport straight from a show in London and drove to the drugstore to pick up Mom's medicine on my way to her house. When I got there, she came downstairs all dressed up and ready to go somewhere.

I asked, "Where are you going?"

She said that she was on her way to her chemo appointment.

"At 7:30 at night?" I asked.

That's when I saw that things were getting worse. She thought it was 7:30 in the morning, not evening. She was starting to get disoriented.

I was overwhelmed with all the touring, the bullshit record-selling-money-hungry world of pressure, and now, most of all, with my mom's illness. I wasn't in a hurry to make another record. I didn't even know if I even wanted to make another record, since I wasn't enjoying what happens after you put out what becomes a popular record. I didn't feel inspired. I had no time to be inspired.

I never considered writing songs about what was going on with my family. On one level, it seemed too personal and too tragic. I didn't think it was something to serve to the world. Then one night while I was lying on the bed in my old room in my mom's basement, I had an epiphany. While I was thinking about all these tragic circumstances, I pictured a blue sky in my head and I suddenly felt greatly inspired. I realized that I *had* to write about what was going on, and that if I didn't it would be like acting and it wouldn't work to try desperately to ignore the ten-ton elephant in the room. And the blue sky told me that there was a way to do this that was something different. That it wasn't all bad, that there was a bright side, even to this. For me, the bright side was knowing that I was going to learn things from all this, and also just the fact that I could be inspired and could do something positive with all of it, and have something to focus on. I could make something from all this.

I could hear so much of it in my head and I was so inspired that I didn't ever consider what a record company might think of what I was about to do. Whenever my mom was stable enough, I'd go back to my house in Echo Park and hole-up in my basement to write and record songs inspired by what had happened and was happening with Liz and my mom. I wanted to honor Liz's memory by telling things from her point of view. One of the things we found after she died was a yellow notepad where a doctor in the mental hospital had asked her to write "I am OK" a hundred times. She wrote it down several times, but then gave up and wrote "I am not OK." What saved me was being able to write these songs. Liz never had that. She felt completely empty and lost. I wanted to give her the gift of making her an artist by putting some of her words inside a musical frame.

Something that had helped Liz for a little while was electric shock therapy. It has a bad rap from the old days, but I guess the modern version of it can really help some people and it did her a lot of good, for a while anyway. I went over to Mickey P.'s, a producer/cut-and-paste computer guy I knew through the Dust Brothers, who lived down the street from me, and we came up with a track that I set some of Liz's experiences to. Some of it was from her own words and some of it I imagined to be how she felt. I called the song "Electro-shock Blues," and decided that would also be a fitting album title.

> *Feeling scared today*
> *Write down "I am OK"*
> *A hundred times the doctors say*
> *I am OK*

I am OK
I'm not OK

I wrote another song from Liz's point of view, but this time about when she was a little kid and things were starting to change for her.

Got a 3 speed and banana seat
Sitting back on the sissy bar
Went to Sev and got a drink
Wish I was driving in Daddy's car
And I looked up at the sky last night
And I thought I saw a bomb
And why won't you just tell me what's going on?

Riding down on Springhill Road
Meeting Alfred out in the woods
Dogs bark and mosquitoes bite
Scratching the itch that makes it feel good
And I looked into the mirror last night
All I saw was a pretty blonde
And why won't you just tell me what's going on?

Those hours down in my basement, or at Mickey's or Jim Jacobsen's or the Dust Brothers' studios, were some of the greatest times of my life. Maybe because everything else was the worst time of my life, the time spent trying to make something positive out of it all was my lifeline. I was really sad anytime I wasn't writing or recording. I just poured myself into it. I didn't have a girlfriend or any kind of a social life, once again. I just wanted to hide from the world and write my little songs, when I wasn't back east looking after my mom.

While out on a tour, I was sitting on my hotel bed somewhere in the French countryside one afternoon, thinking about my mom and our relationship over the years and the way I'd turned out as a person. I picked up my acoustic guitar and started singing:

> *Hate a lot of things*
> *But I love a few things*
> *And you are one of them*
> *Hard to believe*
> *After all of these years*
> *But you are one of them*

It felt good to acknowledge my complicated relationship with my mom, but also to know that I didn't have to be mad at her forever for some of my problems in life that may have resulted from my childhood.

Back at my mom's house, I spent most of the nights after she went to sleep just standing in the dark outside of her house, the house I grew up in, trying to get away from the pain of what was happening inside it. I came back to Echo Park and wrote the saddest song I'd ever written.

> *Standing in the dark outside the house*
> *Breathing in the cold and sterile air*
> *Well I was thinking how it must feel*
> *To see that little light*
> *And watch it as it disappears*
> *And fades into*
> *And fades into the night*

But, even though it was sad, I wanted it to be a wake-up call for those of us who were still alive and kicking.

> *And the streets are jammed with cars*
> *Rockin' their horns*
> *To race to the wire*
> *Of the unfinished line*

The blue sky I had envisioned came out for me one night when I was lying in my cramped bedroom in Echo Park. I was listening to the sounds of the city outside my open window and thinking about how dangerous the neighborhood was, and also about all the things I was learning about life and death. I had become acutely aware of the fact that I was a living, breathing person, and that it was not always going to be that way. I suddenly felt inspired and got out of bed. I went into the living room and picked up the electric baritone guitar leaning against the coffee table and plugged it into an amp and strummed while I started singing.

> *Laying in bed tonight I was thinking*
> *And listening to all the dogs*
> *And the sirens and the shots*
> *And how a careful man tries*
> *To dodge the bullets*
> *While a happy man takes a walk*
>
> *And maybe it is time to live*

I didn't give a shit any more about the MTV world that I had become a part of. I thought it would be cool but, if you saw how it all really works, it's sickening. What if a painter had to show a sketch to a "focus group" before he made a painting?

My manager, Carter, had become like a father figure to me. I didn't realize that I needed one but, obviously, I did. I looked up to him and always took his criticism, which could be brutal, and his approval to heart. When I came over to his house one day to play him some of the *Electroshock Blues* songs, with titles like, "Going to your Funeral" (parts 1 & 2), "Cancer for the Cure," and "Hospital Food," my heart sank as he made it clear that he didn't like the new songs. "Nobody wants to hear an album about *death*," he said.

I went home and thought about his reaction. Carter had been a great manager—he was the first to believe in me and was so instrumental in the success that had finally come. So the fact that he did not believe in my new material was a bad situation for me—because I really believed in it. I was someone who was always doubting himself, and if Carter said something was no good, I discarded it and tried again. But this time I felt, for the first time in my life, like I really knew what I was doing. Everything seemed clear and focused to me in my blue sky. I was sure this was a beautiful thing I was doing, beyond the usual mechanics of the record business. All of the people dying around me were making me keenly aware of how fleeting life on Earth was, and it magnified what was important in the bigger picture. I might as well try to make something good and lasting while I'm here, I thought. I gotta try.

As good a manager as Carter was (and still is), I realized that I was going into uncharted territory to some degree and that it just wasn't something he could be expected to understand how to deal with. I had a lot of sleepless nights over what to do but, ultimately, I knew that I had outgrown my relationship with Carter. My artistic need was now bigger than my need for a surrogate parent. I felt like I was becoming an artist. A real artist, hopefully, and I made a conscious decision that *that* was the priority, not having hits and selling records, like everyone around me seemed so concerned about. You could say that the day I had to fire Carter was the day I finally became a man, in a way. He was understanding and very civil about the whole thing. We've remained friends ever since and I still go to him for business advice on occasion.

In between trips back and forth to Virginia, I finished the album over a period of a few months. I called Lenny at the record company and told him that I had a new album that I wanted to play for him. He was surprised and said he didn't know that I'd even started a new album. I told him that I'd been doing it myself and wanted to keep it organic, rather than the usual method of having the label book and pay for a studio and be involved in the creative process along the way.

I drove my truck to the company headquarters on the other side of town. As usual, the security guard mistook me for a delivery boy as I entered the building. I said hello to Lenny's assistant, Gayle, and she took me to the conference room where Lenny, Mo Ostin, and a few others had gathered. I said hello, told them I was about to play them the new EELS album and that it was something different, it was not *Beautiful Freak Vol. 2*. I explained a little bit of what the album was about. I was nervous, but I also had a new, blind confidence. I was proud of what I had made.

I handed the DAT tape to Lenny and he put it in the

conference room's DAT machine and hit the play button. For the next forty-eight minutes we all sat there on the conference-room couches and listened. Lenny got into his intense "listening to music" stance: leaning forward, his face down in his hands, gently rocking back and forth, occasionally surfacing from his hands in between tracks to say, "Wow . . ." or nod his head from side to side, as if to say, "Man, I can't believe that."

Halfway through the album playback, a song called "Last Stop: This Town," inspired by my landlady Francis's apparition sighting, started playing. Lenny looked up from his hands and smiled as the harpsichord chimed along with drum loops, scratching, and a boys' choir.

> *You're dead but the world keeps spinning*
> *Take a spin through the world you left*
> *It's getting dark a little too early*
> *Are you missing the dearly bereft?*

When it was over, everyone was smiling. I stood up and Lenny reached his hand out to shake my hand.

"Thank you," he said.

"Brilliant, E," Mo chimed in.

I walked out to my truck, started it up, drove a few blocks down Third Street and pulled over so I could start crying. All the pain and drama of the last year was coming out. And, after having to make the extremely tough decision of firing someone who had become a father figure to me, who said no one would want to hear the record, I felt a great sense of not being so alone. Like I wasn't completely crazy. These record executives actually loved music and artistry—these were the guys who signed Neil Young, Jimi Hendrix, Prince, The Kinks, Van Morrison, Randy Newman—and who worked with so many more of my favorite, most respected artists, from Frank Sinatra to Ray Charles. I knew they knew right away it wasn't something that was going to light up the charts or be easy to sell, but they loved it and appreciated what I had given them for what it was.

To me, it wasn't a record about death. That was missing the point. It was about life. And death was a big part of life that tended to be ignored, or denied. No one wanted to think there would be an end to themselves, but I couldn't ignore it, and I realized that if you treat it like the everyday fact of life that it is, it becomes less scary. And also, by being more aware of death, you gain a perspective on living and how you'd better make it count, whatever that may mean to you.

When I made the choice not to let anything get in the way of my new mission to try to be the best artist I could be, I was also setting myself up for a never-ending sequence of lonely battles, as well as branding myself with an ever-increasing reputation for being "difficult" in the eyes of the music industry. Not an easy lifestyle. But if I hadn't made that decision, and instead went along with the cookie-cutter music-business thinking, I would have had to do everything in the name of making executives and shareholders happy by trying to figure out what *they* wanted to hear. There's no happy ending to that story: either you fail and go back to work at the garage, or you succeed and spend the rest of your life hating the whore that you've become. It's hard not being able to be everyone's friend when you decide that your music is your best friend and that you'll do anything to look out for it, but it was the only decision that made any real sense to me. And, amazingly, my first true test of these waters was looking pretty good. I went out on a limb, and Lenny and Mo said the limb wasn't going to break. They didn't ask me to change a single thing about the record, a rare thing from a major record label. They seemed to intuitively respect it and they felt that it was an important record, regardless of its commercial prospects.

During the months between finishing the album and its release later in the year, I spent a lot of time in Virginia, where my mom was getting worse. I arranged for hospice care and they brought a hospital bed and set it up in the dining room where the table usually was, so my mom wouldn't have to go up and down the stairs so much. She was starting to get pretty shaky. We spent a lot of time talking. I realized that if there was anything I'd ever want to know about the family, these were my last chances to find out. All my grandparents had long since died. This was the end of the line.

She decided that it was time to plan her funeral. She wasn't dramatic about it at all. Just matter-of-fact, like it was just another task at hand. I took out a pad of paper and wrote down what she wanted: simple service at the church on Lewinsville Road, some hymns she liked and no testimonials, just the music. Her last wish was for the organist to play the old Roy Rogers song "Happy Trails" at the end of the service, as everyone walked out.

> *Happy trails to you*
> *Until we meet again . . .*

I thought this last touch was genius.

I spent a lot of time playing the piano, behind the dining room where she was lying in her hospital bed. One afternoon I was playing a song I had written years earlier that I never believed was something that had reached its full potential. When I finished, I walked into the dining room and asked my mom if she needed anything.

"Just more of that," she said.

That convinced me that the song was something I should believe in and pursue in the future.

In addition to an African hospice nurse, whom my mom was so fond of that she would kiss goodnight each night, my mom now also had an Iranian woman named Miriam living in the house as a boarder, who happened to be a doctor that worked at a nearby hospital. That was a real godsend, having a doctor in the house. So, whenever I'd go back to California, I knew there was a doctor and a nurse looking after my mom. She'd usually let me know when she was ready to get rid of me and tell me to go back to my life for a little while.

I flew back to LA and my landlady's son came over to my house right after he saw me get out of the taxi. He stood at my door and told me that his mom, Francis, the apparition watcher, had died the night before. She had a bowl of ice cream and then laid down and died. An ambulance came but they couldn't revive her. In the 1930s she used to live in the little house I was now living in. She and her late husband used to have dance parties in the basement where my little studio was now set up. She told me all this one day while I was going through her 78rpm record collection in her basement.

The time came for *Electro-shock Blues* to be released and for me to go on tour again. The hospice nurse and Miriam, the doctor of the house, assured me that my mom was fine and stable. She was still up and about, gardening in the yard, etc., on her good days.

This time I traded my Wurlitzer electric piano for a Hammond organ, which I thought would be better suited to play some of the new stuff, along with the usual electric guitar I was now getting pretty confident at playing. Butch and I hooked up with a guitar-player friend of mine, Adam Siegel, to play bass for the tour. Butch and I weren't getting along very well with Tommy, the bass player, and we agreed that we didn't want to continue with him. Tommy was a nice guy and we had a lot of fun sometimes, but there was something about him that was always rubbing people in our caravan the wrong way. He was young and maybe he was just having a hard time dealing with all the excitement. Adam turned out to be an extraordinary bass player who added a new wallop to our live sound, and he was also a pleasure to be around on a daily and nightly basis.

The album came out to much critical acclaim and the shows went well. It was fun challenging myself by playing the organ as the primary instrument at a rock concert. The shows were difficult for me, due to the subject matter of the new songs, but ultimately it was cathartic and I found myself feeling lighter after every show.

We were invited to play at Neil Young's annual benefit concert for the Bridge School in Northern California. This was always one of the coolest shows of the year, and everyone wanted to be part of it because of Neil Young. The night before the concert, Neil invited all the bands to come to his house for a barbecue. After all of those years of listening to Liz play his records over and over, her taking me to his mind-blowing *Rust Never Sleeps* concert when I was fifteen, and giving Liz his latest album every year for

Christmas or her birthday, I couldn't believe I was meeting the man himself, in his home.

"Hi, E. Nice to meet you," Neil said, shaking my hand.

I was extremely nervous. My mouth was dry. I was in some kind of hyperreality state. My voice cracked, "I like your beard!"

I like your beard? That's what I said to Neil Young. This was one of my first lessons about meeting my heroes. Avoid it when possible, because I have a social dysfunction where I just get too nervous and say something crazy. I don't act like myself. I just lose it and blurt out ridiculous things. It's an extreme version of what I do around people in general, so I tend to like staying at home alone whenever possible to avoid this kind of thing. I would go on to meet more of my heroes in years to come and I got a little better at calming myself down sometimes, but I still always said something stupid because I was so nervous.

Meeting Neil and playing at his concert was a bittersweet experience. It was an honor and so exciting, but I kept wanting to pick up the phone to call Liz and tell her that I was in Neil Young's house or that Neil had just introduced me on stage. She would have freaked out if I put him on the phone. It was so sad to be in the presence of Neil and not be able to tell Liz.

I started to get, and still do get, a lot of mail and comments from people telling me how much *Electro-shock Blues* helped them. When I was younger, I remember trying to make a deal with God where, if he'd let me make music, I'd try to help people. I, of course, had forgotten about this, but now it suddenly dawned on me that both ends of the bargain were being held up simultaneously. According to these letters, I was helping people *by* making music. I didn't have this in mind when I made *Electro-shock Blues*, but I was very happy if it did help people. It was a great feeling.

During a break in the tour, I went back to Virginia. When I got there it was clear that my mom had gotten much worse. She was now bedridden most of the time and was on a lot of morphine to kill the pain. I took over from the hospice nurse and Miriam and became my mom's nurse so they could have a break for a couple of weeks. There was a clipboard with a very complicated schedule of which drugs to give her at which hour and half-hour. She was starting to hallucinate and would do things like ask me to erase the writing on the dining-room curtains.

I slept on the living-room couch a few yards away from my mom's hospital bed in case she needed anything during the night. One night I woke up to the sound of running water. I rolled over and sat up. My mom was squatting on the floor, lifting up her nightgown, and pissing on the carpet. When she was finished, I stood up, walked over and put my hand out to help her back to bed. She had the look of a confused, lost child in her eyes. It was horrible.

I had set up the little black-and-white TV from her bedroom on a hospital-bed table that could swing over her bed so she could watch it. It's hard to shake the heartbreaking image of my mother, bald and emaciated, lying in bed on some of the last Friday nights of her life watching *Sabrina the Teenage Witch*.

One night I was dead asleep on the couch when I heard her calling me.

"Mark? Mark?"

I crawled off the couch and ran over to the dining room. She had shit in her bed and didn't know what to do. I pulled her nightgown off and cleaned up the shit all over her and the sheets. I thought about all the times she must have done this for me when I was a baby, so it only seemed fitting for me to do it for her now. If firing Carter hadn't made me a man, this surely did.

It was all so hard to bear, particularly because this was a woman who prided herself on being active and doing things, always helping out others, never asking for help for herself. I don't remember her spending a single day sick in bed, until she got cancer. She was always out and about, doing something. You could see that she was deeply ashamed of being so helpless.

Thankfully, she started to improve a little. She became more lucid and even started getting out of bed to walk around her garden again. I had a short tour of the U.S. coming up. The hospice nurse returned and said it was a good time for me to go back on tour as my mom was going to be stable for a while.

A couple of weeks later the tour came to Washington, D.C. The last time we did this my mom came to the show, but that clearly wasn't an option anymore. We played the show and I rented a car to drive over to my mom's house to stay for a few days before flying across the country to Seattle to resume the tour.

While I was there, she was doing well. She had her thoughts together and was unusually aware. We talked a lot and it seemed like she was in good shape, all things considered. After a couple of days, I had to go and finish the tour with a few West Coast dates. The hospice nurse told me that my mom would be stable until at least Christmas, a month and a half away, so it wasn't a problem to do these few dates. I flew across the country to meet the band.

When I got to Seattle, I immediately got a call from the hospice nurse saying that I'd better come back to Virginia. As soon as I'd left, my mom's condition had greatly worsened. The nurse said she thought my mom had been looking forward to seeing me and that's what kept her going and in good shape. I went straight back to the airport and flew back across the country. Lisa Germano, our opening act on the tour, became the headliner at our Seattle show that night and explained that there was an emergency keeping the EELS from performing.

When I got to the house, my mom had just suffered a stroke and was slipping into a coma. One side of her face was drooping, and she would occasionally make these little involuntary yelps. It was a horror show. I've never seen anything so horrible before or since. Miriam, the nurse, and I sat around the bed, taking occasional shifts through the night so we could each get a little sleep. Early in the morning, as the sun was coming up, the "death rattle" began and the nurse said, "This is it." Her breathing began to get extremely labored and the low rumble in her lungs was getting louder and louder. I held her hand and talked to her, unsure if there was any use in it. I told her that we were all there for her and how much we loved her. Eventually her breathing began to slow down until it was very, very slow. And then there was one last, slow exhale with no inhale after it.

It hit me hard. Even though I had known it was coming for some time, my mother had just died, right in front of me. I laid my head on her lap and wept uncontrollably. It was November 11, my father's birthday.

It wasn't just that she had died, but the way she died. Watching her fall apart slowly over the last months was bad enough, but the rapid decline of her last night was so horrifying that I can't allow myself to think about it for more than a second.

Now I was all alone in the house I grew up in with my family. They were all gone. The nurse called for a hearse to come and, this time, when they brought out the black bag, I knew to go upstairs and close the door. I wasn't going to watch my mother be carried out the front door in a bag the way I watched my father go.

I canceled the last three shows of the tour and called the minister of my mom's church, who I had already been planning the funeral with. We set the date for a few days later and I checked into a motel off Route 7. I couldn't stay in the house anymore. It was just too sad and lonely for me to sleep there ever again.

Going through my mom's bills, I noticed that the hospice nurse had been making expensive daily calls to her family in Africa from my mom's phone. When I called the hospice about it, no one could find the nurse. She took advantage of a dying woman, chalked up a phone bill in the thousands, kissed her goodnight every night, and vanished.

———

I BUCKLED MY RENTAL CAR'S SEAT BELT AROUND the box of my mom's ashes and drove her to the church. I had to keep thinking of her as being there. I wasn't ready to let go of her. At the funeral, I sat in the front row bawling and blowing snot in wadded-up tissues, while the minister spoke briefly about my mom. Then he said, "Even though she didn't want people to speak about her, would anyone like to?"

People awkwardly held their hands up and told anecdotes about her, even though it was against her wishes. I didn't get it. As the minister signaled that it was time for us to stand up and leave, I didn't recognize the music the organist was playing. Where the fuck is "Happy Trails"? I thought. I got to the church entrance where the minister was standing, and, with tears welling in my eyes, asked him: "What happened to 'Happy Trails'?"

"Oh, yes. We couldn't find the sheet music for it."

I felt like punching the motherfucker right there in his church. The last thing my mom asked for, someone that never asked for much, and you *couldn't find the sheet music*? How fucking hard can it be? You could have started by calling me, because my mom had the sheet music sitting right there on her upright piano. Her last wish, and what would have been a great moment for her and the rest of us, went ungranted.

12
ESTATE SALE

"THAT COULD BE THE NEXT HITLER FOR ALL WE know."

I had just witnessed a death, right before my eyes, and now I was on the other end, witnessing the birth of a friend's baby. We were all huddled around the dark green Hefty bag that was catching the blood and goop spewing out from between the legs of our friend who was currently in the throes of squeezing out her baby in a sterile, fluorescent-lit hospital room. The sun was setting through the Venetian blinds as the women all cried and the men were "high-fiving." I looked around at all the celebrating and it occurred to me that no one knew how this baby was going to turn out as a person.

I leaned over to my girlfriend, who was weeping tears of joy, and whispered into her ear.

"That could be the next Hitler for all we know."

She looked at me in disbelief and curled her mouth into a frown. She wiped the tears away so she could roll her eyes and make an even more disapproving face as she spoke.

"What's *wrong* with you?"

It wasn't that I was so cynical. I just couldn't help but think of all the possibilities, and imagined that one night people were celebrating and doing whatever the 1889 version of high-fiving was as, unbeknownst to them, the world's most horrible monster came into being.

I stood back and watched everyone crying and high-fiving. I looked at the little human that had just popped out of my friend's vagina, all covered in goo.

"Welcome to Earth," I imagined telling the baby. "You're at Kaiser Permanente on Hollywood Boulevard, one of the most depressing stretches of road in the world. Hope you like it."

———

I NOW HAD WHAT FELT LIKE AN IMPOSSIBLY huge and harrowing task to deal with: cleaning out the house I had grown up in with my family, who had all left me behind. By this point I was getting used to just pulling up my bootstraps (whatever that means) and taking care of the task at hand, however grisly it may be, but this was a big one. Would I be able to handle going through all the belongings and memories of not only my mom, my dad, and Liz, but also all the shit from my parents' parents, and their parents before them? I couldn't stand to think about it. There was no one left to deal with all this stuff, I was now the official end of the line.

Once again, having a job to do helped me. Just like making the *Electro-shock Blues* album, having a task at hand made it somewhat easier to deal with, but there were unbearably rough moments.

Our roadie, Spider, flew out to Virginia to help me. I slept at my friend Sean's parents' house up the road each night, unable to bear sleeping in the house. Spider tried to sleep in my parents' bedroom, until he heard weird noises one night and propped a broom handle up against the bedroom doorknob, convinced the house was haunted.

The days were spent trying to quickly figure out what could be thrown out and what I should pack into the U-Haul truck Spider would drive back to my house in California. My Aunt Sally, the wife of my mother's brother, Peter, came down from Vermont and my mom and dad's friend Ann came to help out for a few days. My mother was a pack rat to the point of mental illness, so a lot of it was useless boxes of newspapers and junk. But the attic was full of Liz's stuff and stuff I had never seen that belonged to my grandparents, great-grandparents, and so on. Liz's bed-room and my parents' bedroom were like museum pieces. Little had changed since they were all alive and living there.

In the closet that Liz and I used to hang out in when we were kids, I opened a box that was stuffed full of letters. I picked up a letter at random and made the mistake of reading it. It was a letter my mom had written to Liz when she was a little girl who had gone away to camp in Vermont for the first time. My mom was trying to comfort Liz, who was new to leaving home. It was just too sad. There were a lot of moments like this where I was overcome by grief and had to stop what I was doing.

I found a guy in the Yellow Pages who had a store that sold stuff from estate sales. He came over to see if he wanted to buy any of the furniture. It was all crappy, nothing very nice, but it was still hard for me to think about selling my parents' bed for twenty dollars, no matter how old and shitty it was. It wasn't the money but the idea of these memories being so cheap. I told him I couldn't sell any of the stuff for the money he was offering and he thanked me for wasting his time.

The night we finally had the place emptied out, I walked out through the front door of the house. I couldn't help but think about all the years I had walked through that door and how I was now walking out of it for the last time. Spi-der and I got in the U-Haul and drove over to Mr. Smith's, a restaurant in the strip mall on Route 7 that my dad used to like to go to, so we could have a drink in his honor. After dinner, Spider and I got back in the U-Haul and headed north to Vermont, so I could scatter my mom's ashes in the lake where she had spent much of her childhood swimming and canoeing. Spider dropped me off in Vermont and drove the U-Haul back to Los Angeles.

The next day I scooped out a cupful from the box holding my mom's ashes and gave it to my Aunt Sally to bury near my mom's parents' graves out in the woods near the lake. I scooped out a smaller amount and poured it in a little film vial so I could keep it near the little vial of Liz's ashes I had back at my house in Los Angeles. I took the box with the rest of my mom and got in a canoe.

The sun was shining and the sky was blue with a few white clouds as I paddled closer toward the center of the lake. I noticed a few other boats in the vicinity. I got to a place out in the middle that felt like a nice place for her. Suddenly, out of nowhere, the sky got dark and big gusts of wind were blowing. It started raining big, heavy drops that were pelting me like small stones. What I thought would be a touching ceremony between me and my mother turned into a hurried, workmanlike task as I pulled the plastic bag out of the box, opened it, and poured the contents into the lake, the wind blowing much of the ashes back in my face. Nothing about the act felt poetic. Then I noticed that one of the nearby boats was coming toward me. A guy yelled

"Hey!" and I realized that he probably thought I was dumping waste in the lake. I threw the empty bag on the floor of the canoe and began paddling back to shore as fast as I could.

———

I HAD RECENTLY MOVED FROM THE WEIRD LITTLE Echo Park house on the hill I was living in for six years to a house nearby in Los Feliz that had more room for my ever-growing home-recording needs. The new basement wasn't huge, but compared to the tiny space in my Echo Park house it was. A few days after I got back from Vermont, Spider pulled the U-Haul up to my house and we unloaded my mom's upright piano, her bird feeders and bird books, and lots of boxes of family photos and writings that went back through several generations. I set up my mom's best bird feeder in the backyard and began feeding the birds as a way to stay connected to her. I wrote a song called "I Like Birds."

A sweet old Romanian lady named "Birdy" lived directly across the street from my new house. One day when I was getting into my truck out on the street she asked me for a ride to the health food store. This became a routine: I'd give her rides to the health food store where she'd buy a loaf of bread and then sit out front feeding it to the pigeons. When I had to travel, she'd feed Slinky for me. One evening her brother came to my door and told me that Birdy had died and that she had been sick with cancer for years. I had no idea. She never mentioned it once.

Having closed up the house in Virginia, as a means for survival, I felt like I needed to accentuate the positive and try to look at this point in my life as some sort of new beginning. I began writing songs that sometimes reflected the sadness I couldn't help but feel in the aftermath of death, but also the celebration of life. One thing all these deaths made me notice was that I was still alive.

> *Today is a lovely day to run*
> *Start up the car with the sun*
> *Packing blankets and dirty sheets*
> *A roomful of dust and a broom to sweep up*
> *All the troubles you and I have seen*

Another thing all this death was doing to me was giving me a sense of urgency. I became very aware of what little time a person can have on this Earth, and so I felt a real drive toward making something as well as I could, as soon as I could. I started recording in my new basement straight away.

I stayed positive throughout the recording of these new songs, despite having a recording engineer whose sense of humor was frozen in 1985 and would continuously spend the quiet time between takes singing my lyrics in the voice of Eddie Murphy's "Buckwheat" character from *Saturday Night Live*. ("*Watching the movie / the World's gonna end*" from a song I had written called "Daisies of the Galaxy" became "*Watchin' da mooby / Da world's gointa en . . . O tay!*")

Soon I had a new album called *Daisies of the Galaxy* all ready to throw out there to the world. To me it had a bright and breezy quality to it that equaled the joy and heartbreak of watching the birds in my backyard sit on the feeder and take baths in the birdbath on a beautiful, sunny afternoon, but sometimes also suffer a grisly death at the paws of a killer cat (hey, it happens). When I played the album to Lenny, he loved it. Said it was "as good as it gets," and likened it to "a wonderful walk in the park where you're occasionally bitten by a snake."

When Lenny played the album to the rest of the company, there was not as much celebrating. Having just come off the *Electro-shock Blues* album, the radio department was hoping for something extremely upbeat and catchy to play on the radio. Suddenly my excitement was gone as it became clear that they were not happy with the album. This sent me into a deep depression. I had done everything in my power to rise above the succession of tragedies I'd endured and found a way to embrace life again. I loved the album and believed in it exactly as it was. I worked hard to whittle down twenty-eight songs to these fourteen, sequenced in a way that worked as a whole, and now they wanted me to change it. I sat around the house for months in a depressed fog while the album gathered dust on Lenny's desk. I just couldn't imagine it being different. It felt preordained to me.

After a few months, I woke up one morning and walked out into my backyard. "It's a beautiful day. Goddamn right," I thought. I felt a renewed sense of optimism. It didn't come from anywhere, just my need to pull up my bootstraps and move on. I simply *had* to snap out of my funk and start looking forward again. I called Mike Simpson of the Dust Brothers, a frequent collaborator of mine, and asked if he felt like getting together to make a little music. We quickly made a new track that everyone, even the record company, seemed excited about. "Goddamn right, it's a beautiful day." I was coming out of the fog.

> *The smokestack spitting black soot into the sooty sky*
> *The load on the road brings a tear to the Indian's eye*
> *The elephant won't forget what it's like inside his*
>   *cage*
> *The ringmaster's telecaster sings on an empty stage*
> *Goddamn right, it's a beautiful day*

The record company wanted to add the new song, called "Mr. E's Beautiful Blues," to the album immediately. I really believed in the album and wanted people to hear it. Having watched it sit on the shelf gathering dust for seven months now, I decided that my only real choice was to try to comply with the label's wishes, so I went to work at resequencing the album to include it. But it seemed to ruin the album, no matter where I put it. I liked it as a song, but I just couldn't get it to keep from disrupting the flow of the album. Dejected, I gave up. The album was good the way it was, I was certain.

The record company insisted the song be included and the only idea I could think of was to tack it on to the end of the album as a "bonus track," which was becoming a new trend that I didn't particularly care for. At least it wouldn't disrupt the flow of the album before it. I asked them to put ten seconds of silence between the last track of the album, "Selective Memory," and the new bonus track. Then, at the last minute, I called the mastering lab myself and had them sneak in another ten seconds so there would be twenty seconds of silence after what I considered the perfect ending of the album and before this bonus track came blaring on.

Lenny called me one day to tell me that a new film called *Road Trip* wanted to use the new song for a sequence in the film. Not only that, but they wanted to make a video for the song, and they'd pay for it. I was totally against this idea. I had been happy to have my songs in some films, like *American Beauty* and Wim Wenders's *The End of Violence*, but I didn't want this brand-new song to be associated with a frat-boy movie, of all things. That's not a beautiful day, and not a good first impression for my new song and album. But I was told, in no uncertain terms, either put the song in the film, do the video, or forget about us letting anyone know your new record exists—it may not ever come out.

They made me be in a humiliating video where I drove a bus full of the film's actors around. I felt like an idiot. The only good part about it was when they shot a scene of me beating the shit out of some of them. To this day, I've never seen the film but I know it's not what I wanted to do as an artist at that time with that song, and it's something I still regret. Maybe I'm lucky because I don't have a lot of things I regret. I never regretted all the commercials I had turned down. The feeling of maintaining my integrity was worth more than the millions of dollars I was passing up, I knew this for sure.

And, of course, it was all for nothing, anyway. When the song was released, we quickly learned that American radio doesn't like the term *goddamn* and my song had twelve of them in it. I also learned that you can't say "goddamn" even on late-night TV in America, when the producers of *The David Letterman Show* forbade me from singing "Mr. E's Beautiful Blues" because the CBS censors will allow the word *God* and the word *damn* to be used separately, but never together. Instead, we played another song from the album and I ad-libbed a little tribute to the censored rock heroes of the Ed Sullivan stage that I was performing on that evening.

"Let's spend some time together" (Mick Jagger eye-roll)/ *"Girl we couldn't get much . . . HIGHER!"* (Jim Morrison bellow).

And it got even more ridiculous. The campaign to elect the tragically inept Republican candidate George W. Bush to the White House used the *Daisies of the Galaxy* album as an example of the entertainment industry marketing smut to children. I know. Pretty hilarious. I was thrilled by it, of course. We were being mentioned in the front news section of *The Washington Post*. It was all so utterly ridiculous. The CD had a storybooklike cover and had song titles such as "It's a Motherfucker" (which was actually a tender ode to the hardships of missing the girlfriend I had recently broken up with) and, of course, the "goddamn" song, so they deduced that the storybook cover meant it was targeted for three-year-olds or something. It was great. You could download my lyrics from the "George W. Bush For President" website.

> *It's a motherfucker*
> *Being here without you*
> *Thinking 'bout the good times*
> *Thinking 'bout the bad*
> *And I won't ever be the same*

> *It's a motherfucker*
> *Getting through a Sunday*
> *Talking to the walls*
> *Just me again*
> *But I won't ever be the same*
> *I won't ever be the same*

It's a motherfucker
How much I understand
The feeling that you need someone
To take you by the hand
And you won't ever be the same

You won't ever be the same

I had written this song on a very lonely Sunday afternoon. I was really missing my ex-girlfriend and getting through the weekend was excruciating. I had nothing to do and I was trying to do anything to get through the day. I walked to a movie theater and sat alone in an aisle seat, thinking it would be a good way to pass a couple of hours. Just before the film started, the woman sitting in front of me said, "Since you're ALONE, could you move seats?"

It was one of those kind of days.

Another offending lyric that the Bush campaign presented to the press was from a song called "Tiger in My Tank," an anticommercial "jingle" I wrote:

When I grow up I'll be
An Angry Little Whore

This was from a verse about the so-called alternative culture and how it was just fashionable to appear as a rebel, but nothing else, no real rebellion, was needed. But in the hands of the humorless right-wing conservatives, it was to be taken *literally*, as if I was telling small children to aspire to be prostitutes as soon as they were old enough and, in the case of "It's a Motherfucker," to have intercourse with their mothers? I'm not one for politically correct, mealy-mouthed, obvious rock singers preaching to the choir, but even I had to marvel at what idiots these people were. *The Washington Post* reported:

> *Bush campaign spokesman Ari Fleischer said the combination of the obscene words and child-friendly jacket "shows that America's families and parents cannot count on Al Gore to stop Hollywood from marketing this stuff to children."*

Ari Fleischer is the guy who told America to "watch what you say" a year later. So much for the Bill of Rights.

A few years after winning the election, Vice President Dick Cheney, who had taken part in the *Daisies of the Galaxy*=smut debacle, exploded at Vermont senator Patrick Leahy, telling him to go fuck himself during a heated exchange on the Senate floor. After his outburst, Cheney noted that he felt better after saying it.

Fuck him.

13

I'M MAD AT YOU/ NINA SIMONE IS DEAD

"YOU ARE NOT BEAUTIFUL."

I'm sitting in a salad factory somewhere in Germany and a pretty Russian woman just turned to me and said, "You are not beautiful."

———

BACK BEFORE I LEFT LOS ANGELES, BUTCH THE drummer called me one morning. "Milkman, I had a dream last night that we were on stage with horns and string players. We were playing the new songs. It was beautiful."

Butch had adopted the use of the nickname our old Echo Park friend Alan had given me. It was time to go back out and play music for people again. Butch called to tell me about this idea that had come to him the night before. I loved the idea of expanding the onstage lineup to include instruments we hadn't had before. We quickly went from the three-piece band we were on the last tour to a six-piece band, where we all traded instruments among one another. There were acoustic and electric guitars, an upright acoustic piano, mandolin, banjo, violin, saxophone, flute, clarinet, trombone, trumpet, melodica, glockenspiel, timpani, and a drum set—all being handled at different times by six people.

After all the "death-rock" of the last tour, it was important to me to put on a show that felt blatantly full of life. We started many of the shows with an overture of EELS songs of the past done in wildly different arrangements from the original versions, which segued into our take on Nina Simone's version of the old show tune "Feeling Good," complete with trombone and baritone saxophone honking away, ushering in the new songs and attitude. When we played "Susan's House" now, it had completely new lyrics and a message about forgiveness. Some nights the shows felt closer to a Broadway play than a rock concert. It was joyous.

Shortly before the release of the *Daisies of the Galaxy* album, we all flew to England to perform on some TV shows.

After the last TV performance there were two weeks of nothing scheduled before the European concert tour started, so everyone flew back to America to be with their loved ones. I didn't have any loved ones, so I didn't see the point in going all the way back to America just long enough to get used to normal sleeping hours in a vastly different time zone, only to then come all the way back again.

I hadn't been feeling well since the late '80s. Just kind of run down and crappy-feeling. There was a distinct moment when it hit me: I was riding my bike home from one of my shitty jobs when all of the sudden I felt terrible and had to get off my bike and push it the last two miles home. Ever since then, I hadn't felt right. It never went away. I was pretty used to it at this point, and had tried everything. Almost.

My kooky new-age doctor to the stars in Los Angeles had told me about an even kookier doctor in Germany, who wasn't actually a doctor but a guy who was supposed to be great at recharging people's batteries after feeling run down. Although skeptical, I also always kept an open mind to possibilities and, besides, I didn't have anywhere else to go for two weeks, so I decided to go see this guy out in the country somewhere outside of Hamburg until the European tour started.

I walked off the little propeller plane in Hamburg and met the "doctor" with the crazy, long white beard, who had come to pick me up. He explained that there would only be one other patient while I was there, a Russian woman who had lived near Chernobyl when the nuclear accident occurred, whom I would meet the next day. I imagined I'd be spending the next two weeks sitting next to a charming old Russian milkmaid. I would try not to focus on the hair sprouting from the big mole on her nose as she nodded and smiled at me, never understanding a word I said.

The next morning I woke up in a cold old castle. The castle had been turned into a hotel and I was the only guest currently staying in it. The "doctor" rented me one of his cars. I drove it over to . . . the salad factory. It turned out that he ran a little factory that packaged organic salads and then had this business of recharging people's batteries on the side, all in the same building. I sat down at a desk in the drafty office and was instructed to mix up a giant pile of vitamin C powder into a bottle of water. Then my fingers were hooked up to electrodes that were supposedly giving off tiny electrical currents that would kill parasites in my body. As I gulped down the vitamin C mix with my electrode-wired fingers clamped around the bottle, the front door of the factory suddenly opened and the freezing wind of the German winter came gushing in. Then a very pretty girl walked in.

"Oh, Mark," the "doctor" said, "this is Anna. How do you feel today, Anna?"

"Prer-fect!" exclaimed the pretty girl in cute Russian-accented broken English, her eyes beaming out of her skull. "I walked the whole way here!"

She sat down at the desk next to me as I studied her green eyes, roman nose, full lips, and long, light brown hair. I distinctly ran the words *this is the most beautiful girl in the world* through my head. I felt a wave of anxiety wash over me as I suddenly realized that I wasn't going to be able to relax on this trip. She had already been there for a week and sat down and started hooking up her fingers to the electrodes that were lying on the desk next to mine. As salad-packing employees scurried around us, she turned to me and blurted "YOU ARE NOT BEAUTI-FUL."

She didn't have a typical Russian accent. Not like the Boris and Natasha cartoons or any other Russian person I had ever spoken to before. She sounded like she was from her own planet. I loved her blunt and direct nature. How refreshing. Such a change from all the bullshit American phonies, I thought to myself.

Although she was blunt, she also possessed a complete lack of pretense. She grew up extremely poor, had to flee her village after the Chernobyl accident, and put herself through school to become a dentist. She was, in some ways, very simple. But in other ways, extremely complicated. I was smitten, of course.

She was staying in the "doctor's" mother-in-law's house a couple of miles down the snowy road from the salad factory. The "doctor" could see that we were hitting it off and asked me if I wanted to move from the lonely castle hotel into his mother-in-law's house where Anna was staying. "Yes!" I immediately answered.

I moved my stuff over to the little house that evening. There were three bedrooms: one for Anna, one for me, and one for the mother-in-law, whose room was in between our two rooms. We became inseparable, constantly sneaking back and forth into each other's rooms whenever we weren't at the salad factory.

Two weeks later I left the clinic, not feeling any physically different from when I had arrived, but feeling quite different emotionally. As far as I could tell, the "doctor" was, indeed, a quack—my body didn't feel any better, but I did get a girlfriend out of it, so I wasn't complaining. I met up with the band back in London and told them all about this new development. Anna was splitting her time living between Moscow and London, and she had a six-month visa that allowed her to come and go to England as she pleased, so whenever I was in England would be my only chance to see her. Being a Russian citizen meant that seeing her anywhere else would be extremely complicated, difficult or impossible. She would ride around England on the bus with us, having a great time. She was the single most unique personality I'd ever met. Everyone was charmed by this unusual, strange, and beautiful girl. She put ketchup on French toast and mayonnaise on burritos (really). When it got late and it was time to go to bed, she wouldn't yawn and crawl off to bed like most people. She'd grab my arm and exclaim, "LET'S SLEEP!" She'd always make a special trip by our roadie Spider's bunk to say, "Goodnight, Spider!" in her cute Russian-tinged English.

Luckily we were doing a lot of shows in England that year, but when we went to other places there was no way for me to see her. It would take months to get visas for her to go to different countries, and even then you didn't know if they'd come through. The Russian consulate was notoriously unpredictable and untrustworthy. This was going to pose a problem once I went back to America as well. We went on to tour Europe, America, and Australia and I started to miss her terribly.

We played our last two shows in Australia, two nights at the Atheneum, a great old theater in Melbourne, and had a day off before flying to Japan for some shows. I woke up in the hotel in Melbourne and plugged the phone in. The message light started blinking. The message was from a guy at the record company asking if I wanted to be on a couple of TV shows that day and that, although it was my day off, it would really mean a lot to them if I would appear. I didn't have anything to do, as usual, so I called him back and agreed.

On the second TV show, a national live talk show, they asked me what I thought of Australia and I joked that I loved it because the weather was nice and the heroin was great. In truth, I'd never tried heroin. We weren't a drug band. I had heard that Melbourne was known for having a real heroin problem and very strong heroin, so I made a joke about it.

When I returned to the hotel that evening Butch was sitting in the lobby.

"Milkman, come with me, we have to talk."

He gestured for me to follow him to the elevator. God-damnit, not the "we have to talk" thing. This is never, ever good.

"What's going on?" I begged to know.

"Let's just get upstairs."

The elevator doors opened and we walked down the hall to Butch's room. He slid the card into the slot, opened the door, and sat on his bed. I stood there.

"Spider's dead."

It sounded so ridiculous and I couldn't really soak it in. We had just done a show the night before and he was fine and in great spirits.

"What?"

"Spider's *dead*. He died today."

"*What?* How?"

"We don't know, maybe a heart attack. They found him on the floor of his room."

"Shit. Really? How could that be true?"

We canceled the Japanese shows and made plans to go straight home. The police came and interviewed each of us individually to compare notes. It turned out that a man had been seen with Spider earlier in the day who was then seen fleeing from the hotel, and there was powder found under Spider's nose. Spider was not a drug guy. He was a raging alcoholic who was going through a clean and sober period after getting fired as a result of being so drunk that he fell flat on his face in the aisle of a plane he and Butch were on. He had been doing great for many months since and was rehired. But it looked like maybe he got together with an old friend in Australia and had some heroin and, since he wasn't someone who used it often, if ever, he must not have realized how much he was taking, or how strong it was, and it killed him. Suddenly, my joke on TV a few hours earlier wasn't so funny.

We were all in a state of shock. The police were very nice and understanding. We made arrangements to have Spider's body flown back to America and later we had a little memorial get-together in his honor. Spider's mom was a tiny eighty-year-old woman who lived near Boston. To make me laugh, whenever we played in Boston, Spider would have her on the side of the stage and get her to pass my guitars to me between songs. I'd go over to grab a guitar from Spider but, instead, I'd see the smallest little old lady in the world wearing one of my guitars and reaching out to me with another. She came out to our memorial for him and sat there while we reminisced about him. Butch tried to tell a story about Spider but started blubbering like a baby. We watched videos of Spider singing his songs and telling jokes from some of the shows where he performed as our opening act. It was painful to see him so alive, talking like he was right there in the room with us. Back at home, even if I didn't want to think about him, whenever something broke that needed to be fixed, I would quietly get angry at Spider for his adventure the last day of his life. He was the guy who would come over and fix things for me. At this point, I suppose I was getting pretty used to people dying. But I can't say that just because I was getting used to deaths occurring so frequently it made it any easier.

———

THE ODDS OF ANNA GETTING A REGULAR tourist visa to visit America were slim to none. The government makes it very difficult and thinks that everyone just wants to leave Russia forever to live in America. It became apparent that the only way Anna and I could continue to see each other would be to get what is called a "fiancée visa." With a fiancée visa she could come to America if she intended to get married. So the only way we could continue to even see each other at all, really, was to get engaged.

Marriage always seemed like one of those things "normal" people did. It often seemed to me that people did it just because it was what everyone else does. But when I met someone who was so odd and truly unique—from a planet of her own—and knowing that it was the only way we could continue to see each other, the idea started to really appeal to me. This was going to be a weird, fun adventure.

The American consulate accidentally sent the visa to Missouri instead of Moscow, so it took six months before Anna was allowed to come to America. She finally arrived and one of the happiest yet most stressful periods of my life began.

When she got off the plane in Los Angeles, the customs inspector looked at her passport and asked, "And what are you doing in America?" as they ask most arriving passengers. Anna answered, "What am I doing? *LIVING MY LIFE!*"

I had recently started to contribute songs to any film that had a green monster in it. Despite George W. Bush's misdiagnosis, I do like being involved in kid-friendly projects. Kids know what's going on. They always respond to The Beatles, for instance. Doesn't matter when they were born, they always seem to respond. Show me a kid who innately doesn't like The Beatles, and I'll show you a bad seed. On Anna's first night in America, she came with me to the premiere of *The Grinch* film, which I had contributed a song to. I hated going to things like film premieres or award shows, finding that they brought out the worst side of humanity. You're treated like dirt until they realize you're "somebody" and then you see their personalities completely change. I hate to see that, so I stopped going to them whenever I could get out of it. But I thought this would be fun for

Anna's first night. As we walked in the theater, she saw the actor Jim Carrey about to sit in his seat and walked up to him and said, "Hello. We like you in Russia."

One Saturday morning we went to the courthouse and stood in line with eight or nine unhappy-looking pregnant couples to get married. She wore a pretty dress and I wore a suit. None of the other couples were dressed formally. I brought a small, old wind-up gramophone and a copy of the Wedding March I found in my grandparents' collection of 78rpm records. When our turn came, we walked into the courtroom and I set the gramophone on a table and took the lid off it. I cranked the handle several times. As I put the needle on the record, the Wedding March began playing through the crackly 78rpm static and the judge walked Anna down the aisle.

Later, I went to Russia to meet her family and see where Anna had lived. Her parents still lived in the house that she grew up in as a teenager, the one they fled to after Chernobyl. It was a little shack in a gray, muddy village out in the middle of nowhere. You could buy the whole house for five hundred American dollars. There was no hot water and it was cold as shit. But it was really cozy and I slept great there.

The domestic life back at home was fun, much of the time. I was always playing old records on my little record player in the dining room. Bob Dylan, Ray Charles, Nina Simone . . . One day while I was playing *The Freewheelin'*

Bob Dylan for the thirtieth day in a row, Anna was making some tea when she suddenly put the kettle down, turned the stove off, walked over to the record player, and lifted the needle off the record.

"I HATE BOB DEEEE-LANNNNN!"

She did, however, seem to appreciate some of the other records I was playing. She asked if Ray Charles and Nina Simone were still alive. I told her that they were and she said "We have to go see them!" I promised her we'd see both of them the next time they came to town. Ray Charles was coming soon but Nina Simone had just played a concert the year before, so I didn't know how soon she'd come back. I went to that concert with my date, Lauretta, the seventy-five-year-old widow of the great comedic actor Marty Feldman. Seeing the living legends in person can be a great experience. Nina Simone came out that night to a standing ovation and said, "Do you love me?!"

The audiences erupted.

"You *should*!"

Then she bawled out the bass player for playing too busy. It was great.

I took Anna to the park in Pasadena where Ray Charles was giving a free concert one Sunday evening. We sat on a bale of hay and the great man himself walked out right there in front of us and put on a show. Not long after, I heard that Nina Simone was doing a show in Los Angeles again, but that it hadn't even been advertised and sold out immediately. I couldn't believe it. I apologized to Anna for missing this Nina Simone concert and promised we wouldn't miss the next one. I figured that since she had come back so soon after the last one, there'd probably be another show soon enough.

A few months later I turned the TV on one evening and there was a commercial for the upcoming evening news. The newscaster spoke, "Jazz great Nina Simone dies, story at six."

Shit. Now I've really blown it, I thought. I wondered how I was going to break the news to Anna. A few minutes later I heard Anna's car pull up in front of the house. She walked in with her brow furrowed and her mouth puckered, as if she'd just bitten into a sour pear.

"I'm mad at you."

"Why?" I asked.

"Nina Simone IS DEAD!"

It was the happiest time of my life, much of the time. We would have the greatest times. But with the charm of her different personality also came a, well . . . refer to the title of Chapter 9 of this book. Don't make me say it. I mean, come on. As she once pointed out, we met in a salad factory that doubled as a new-age clinic on the outskirts of Hamburg. It might as well have been a mental hospital.

It lasted five or six years. In the end, it didn't work out. But, after all, this is Chapter 13. What did you expect?

14

ROCK HARD TIMES

I'M SITTING ON A TOILET IN AN OUTDOOR BATH-room in the middle of the central California woods, using a pencil tied to the bathroom cleanup-duty clipboard to scribble lyrics on a roll of toilet paper.

At this point in the book, gentle reader, you may notice me shifting into the present tense a little more often, as a lot of the stories I've told you thus far were about what I consider to be more formative experiences, if you will. Whereas we're starting to get into some things that feel closer to my modern times and who I am now. Let's get back to the action, dear reader:

I've taken a break from recording and tragedies to go to a meditation retreat that my ex-girlfriend Susan has told me about. It's way out in the middle of nowhere and you don't speak a word for ten days. You're not allowed to write or read either. It's January and really cold out in the hills. You don't do anything except eat hippie food and learn a Buddhist meditation technique. Most of the time you're just sitting on the floor of a big, drafty room with nothing but your thoughts, which you're trying to stop. You're forced to come face-to-face with how your mind works, because there's nothing else. And you start to feel like you're going crazy for the first few days.

One day during a break, I'm out walking around the woods when I'm startled to see a mountain lion approaching me. He comes right up to me on the trail. I'm scared that he's about to lunge and rip me to shreds to get the cashews he can probably smell that I have hidden in my pocket. (Susan had warned me that they didn't give her enough hippie food, and to sneak some nuts in my pockets.) But he doesn't lunge at me. He approaches me and simply looks up, as if to say, "Hey, how's it going?" and then he casually goes off on his way. It occurs to me that he's been surrounded by gentle meditators for years, which must have squelched his natural violent tendencies. This puts me in a good mood. I go back to the tiny cabin I share with two other guys. It's weird hanging out and sleeping in the same room with two people you've never spoken to and aren't allowed to speak to, but I was trained pretty well for this by being in the same room with my father all those years. I desperately want to tell my cabin mates about the friendly mountain lion, but can't.

While meditating each day, one of the thoughts that keeps coming back in my head, which I'm trying to clear, is a story my friend Sean had recently told me about a serial killer in the San Francisco area who was known as The Soul Jacker. His claim to fame was that he not only bodily killed his victims, but also claimed to steal their souls. I'm thinking about this and I realize that no one can take your soul if you don't let them. You know, if you have a sense of your soul and you don't sell it or let it be tampered with . . . how can anyone take that away from you? I start to run these words through my head to a tune:

> *Souljacker can't get my soul*
> *Ate my carcass in a black manhole*
> *Souljacker can't get my soul*
> *He can shoot me up full of bullet holes*
> *But the Souljacker can't get my soul*

I can't stop running this song through my head. I need to get it out of there so I can clear my mind. I want to call my answering machine back home and sing it onto the tape, but I'm not allowed to speak and there aren't any phones, anyway. One morning while it's still dark out I sneak into the outdoor bathroom across from our cabin. I have recently spotted the only writing utensil I've seen anywhere on the premises in this bathroom. I make sure no one is in there and take the cleanup clipboard into a stall. I sign up to clean the bathroom and then nervously write down the lyrics that have been running through my head for days onto a roll of toilet paper as fast as I can. Suddenly, someone enters the bathroom. I hold my breath and hide the clipboard and toilet paper behind the toilet tank, as if I'm doing drugs in the toilet stall. I'm just trying to write a song.

On the eleventh day of the retreat a great thing happens. They tell us that we get to talk to anyone and everyone for a couple of hours. During the ten days of never talking to my cabin mates, I had developed an idea and attitude in my mind about what they were like and how I didn't really like them and they didn't like me. But then when we actually speak, I'm surprised to find out how completely wrong I was. They're nice guys, who I like a lot, and they seem to like me, too. This is an important lesson for me about how my mind works.

On the drive home I stop to get gas. It feels strange to be back in the real world. As I'm pumping gas, I see the headline on a newspaper in the window of a newspaper machine next to the gas pumps. It says "MONICA LEWINSKY SAID TO HAVE PROOF." I think, "Who the hell is Monica Lewinsky and why is her name so big on the front page of the paper?" I hadn't been exposed to any media for eleven days. The story had broken during these eleven days and she was already a household name to the world.

When I get back to Echo Park, I record the song I wrote on toilet paper onto a little portable cassette recorder and call it "Souljacker Pt. II," knowing that I want to write a part one for it soon, which happens while rehearsing with the band for a tour. I record the "Souljacker Pt. I" song along with other, like-minded songs during the *Daisies of the Galaxy* album sessions after the tour, but I decide that these songs have a certain musical aggressiveness that sets them too far apart from the other songs I'm recording for *Daisies of the Galaxy* and that, rather than make a double album incorporating the louder, more aggressive *Souljacker* songs with the softer, breezier *Daisies of the Galaxy* songs, I'll set the *Souljacker* songs aside and let them be part of their own album in the future. Meanwhile, I'm working on three other albums as well. I finish two of them but decide they're not what I want to put out and the third one is such a huge project in my mind that I tell myself to let it evolve over the years until it's as good as it can be.

When you're a kid and you're watching your favorite band on TV, it just looks fun and exciting. But it turns out that, in reality, to do it, and to try to do it well—really caring about how it turns out—is extremely hard work and a very stressful lifestyle. It's not for anyone who isn't totally devoted to the mission and willing to give up any kind of real life. Because no one will ever care about your stuff as much as you and there will be daily battles to fight—hard, lonely battles. And they never seem to stop for me. Maybe I put too much weight on it because I recognize the fact that music saved my life. Where would I be if I hadn't had it to focus on all this time? Probably off in that parallel universe that my sister went to meet my father in. So I really take it seriously.

After finishing up the *Daisies of the Galaxy* tour, I turned my attention back to the Souljacker songs I had recorded and decided to do some more songs with John Parish, a friendly English gentleman I had met on the set of *Top of the Pops*. He was there playing with PJ Harvey while I was there with my band. We talked and it seemed that we had a similar love of certain sounds that might make people get up to check and see if something was wrong with their stereo. I sent him the song "Souljacker Pt. I" and another one called "Jungle Telegraph" with a few others I had already recorded for the album and told him I wanted to do some more that would fit in with these. He flew over and lived in the little cabin in my backyard for three weeks while we hammered out some more, most of which he had started in his basement in Bristol.

John and I holed-up in my basement with my recording engineer and "beat specialist" Ryan Boesch, and bass and synthesizer player Koool G Murder. Koool G is a laid-back guy with a big red beard who likes to go to restaurants and tell the waiter to surprise him. I adopted this "surprise menu" practice for a while, asking waiters and waitresses to bring me anything on the menu. It seemed like a good way to help remind myself how you can never know what to expect from life. Occasionally it backfires and you get a dish you really don't like, but more often than not I got something I wouldn't have normally ordered that I ended up loving. Koool G finally took the practice too far one night while on tour in Portugal. The restaurant gave us menus that included the following dish, listed as such:

Little fried birds (not recommended).

Because it sounded like the most surprising item on the menu, G ordered it. Soon a plate with, yes, little fried birds—feathers, beaks, and all—was set down in front of him. He ate them. We all watched with disgust as the little fried birds passed through his giant red beard and into his mouth. Koool G didn't look very Koool during the show that night, his blue face now offsetting his red beard. He spent the next three days vomiting.

The combination of the dapperly dressed English John and the very California Koool G, mixed with the extremely Floridian Ryan (think Adam Sandler in Alabama) looked like a disaster of worlds colliding on paper, but actually made for a surprisingly refreshing mix on tape. You couldn't find more disparate people from each other, but we got lucky and our differences in personality and musical background seemed to only complement the music and give it a unique sound. Plus, we were having a lot of fun doing it. We were all excited about these new songs. It felt like we were on to something fresh and new. Getting into a group of people who are having fun and excited about making new music had now become my way of feeling like I was part of some sort of family.

I sequenced twelve of the songs into an album and called it *Souljacker*. This time I was writing a lot of the songs in the voice of different characters, not so much from my own personal point of view. And the music was very loud, electric, and aggressive compared to the *Daisies of the Galaxy* album that had just come out. It was the early days of my marriage, so I found time to throw in some mushy love songs to give the album a little more dimension so that it wouldn't feel too one-sided. And I could make the music accompanying the mushy lyrics so aggressive, like in a song called "What Is This Note?," an experiment in coupling bad schoolboy love poetry with the most unexpected musical accompaniment. That way, the mushy lyrics felt not so mushy, but more like a crazy, high-octane celebration. Or I could give a mushy song a title like "World of Shit" so it didn't feel so mushy:

> *In this world of shit*
> *Baby you are it*
> *A little light that shines all over*

Must take over
And see us through the night

Daddy was a troubled genius
Mama was a real good egg
Why don't we just get together
For whatever
And see if it's alright

I felt like what we had was what I wanted it to be: a dynamic, loud, vital record that may have appeared to be "dark" on the surface, but was really about the sanctity of the human spirit.

The record company, however, didn't share my opinion about the record. It was crushing to hear that they weren't thrilled with it. They had a hard time getting used to my new sound and wanted, like the last time, songs they felt were obvious hits for the radio. I didn't know what that was anymore, if I ever did. I just wanted it to be good.

Times were changing, and things were changing rapidly for the music business. More and more, it seemed, the days of having my hand shaked and being thanked for turning in an album like *Electro-shock Blues* were fast disappearing, replaced by an ever-increasing need to focus on the bottom line: making money, and only making money, quality and artistry be damned. But I had become hypersensitive to what really mattered to me after losing my family and so many people dying around me. And I wasn't about to start compromising now that I had finally gotten to a point where I felt sure of myself and what I was doing.

I was meeting with different managers to oversee the release of the album. They all told me how great they thought the album was until they heard that the record company didn't like it. One was a young know-it-all punk who said I should redo the songs with a producer who could make them hits. I hired another manager who seemed very excited about the album. A week later he called and said he was refunding his commission because I said I wasn't interested in writing more "singles." These were dark days. I felt like I was going crazy. Every time I listened to what we had recorded to see if I could understand what they were so worried about, I never could wrap my head around it. It sounded great to me, and it was exactly what I wanted it to be. Having lost my family, music was more important to me now than it had ever been. It *was* my family now. I poured everything I had into it, so every stumbling block was a debilitating defeat.

The English office of the record company was a little more receptive and set a release date later in the year, while the album gathered dust on the American office's shelf. Before the album came out, we went out on tour. We showed up to play for a gigantic crowd at the Reading Festival, with our new giant beards, loud guitars, thrashing drums, robotic vocoders and synthesizers, playing mostly new songs no one had heard yet and reshaping old songs to the point of being almost unrecognizable. A sea of people stretched out to the horizon stared blankly back at us.

When *Souljacker* was finally released in America the following year, it was heralded by the critics. *Time* magazine called it the best rock record of the year to date, and I'd be lying if I said I didn't feel vindicated after the lukewarm reception the label gave it. So I won't lie. It felt good after all it took to get the damn thing out. Years later, I even have the nerve to look back and say that I think I was right. And everyone who worked on the album continues to get work based on their being part of it. Not to mention how many times the album's cover has been appropriated for other album covers and even a hugely popular video game. So, whatever. Fuck off, everybody. Just let me do my thing, please? I'm not fucking around here anymore, people. I'm gonna hate myself in the morning, but that felt good to say.

Besides the record company not being crazy about *Souljacker,* a lot of our existing fans from the past didn't seem too crazy about it at first either, based on the Reading Festival experience and some others like it. That's the thing about fans. If they like one thing you do, and you don't do the same thing again, they can feel let down. I never understood that way of thinking, so it means nothing to me, sorry. Why on earth would you want everything to be the same all the time? You can go back and listen to *Daisies of the Galaxy* anytime you want to. I don't need to do it again.

That said, I don't set out to dazzle the world with my "versatility." I just have some things in me that need to come out. If you only like one kind of music, sorry again, but life's too short. Every record I've ever put out has been met with some torrent of angry fan mail because it wasn't what they *expected*. If you want what you expect, why not make your own album, then? I'm just trying to make mine, and it's probably not what you're expecting. I'm glad we had this little talk.

The first song I wrote with John Parish for the album was called "Dog Faced Boy." I knew a woman who had told me how she had very hairy arms when she was a kid and the school kids would tease her and call her "Gorilla Girl." She would beg her fundamentalist Christian mother to shave her arms, but her mother refused. Gorilla Girl grew up to be very pretty and had the last laugh. For the song, I changed it to a boy with facial hair, like they used to have at circus freak shows, so I could sing it more convincingly in the first person. I got so into the character that I started to grow a long, wild beard. I also got a very short haircut. The combination made me look unwittingly like a devout Muslim.

> Going back to the school tomorrow
> Hang my hairy head in sorrow
> Ain't no way for a boy to be
> Ain't no way to set me free now

Ma won't shave me
Jesus can't save me
Dog faced boy

On September 11, 2001, I was in London, in the middle of the *Souljacker* tour. I appeared on a morning radio talk show where I debated the host over his negative assessment of the Bob Dylan album that had been released that day by demanding, "Do you really think you know better than Bob Dylan!?"

I went back to the hotel to take a nap. Thirty minutes later, the tour manager called my room and woke me up.

"Have you been watching CNN?"

"No. What's going on?"

"A plane hit the World Trade Center."

I turned on the TV, along with the rest of the world, and watched in horror as the second plane hit the other tower. It was all so surreal, none of us knew what to make of it. I was scheduled to tape a live session with the band at a radio station that afternoon and we decided to go ahead with it. There were all sorts of rumors about other planes on their way to hit other targets and areas. As we set up to play at the radio station we were told there was a rumor that a hijacked plane was on its way to crash into the West End of London, which was where we were. We figured if we're going out, we might as well go out rocking. We sent one of the roadies down to get some beer and proceeded to get drunk and play, wondering if we were about to die at any given moment.

The rumor turned out to be only a rumor. We finished our session and went back to the hotel. I checked my messages in America and heard the voice of my Aunt Sally saying she had some bad news. My cousin Jennifer and her husband were flight attendants on the plane that hit the Pentagon earlier in the day. Usually they don't let married flight attendants work on the same flight, but since they were going to take a vacation in LA at the end of the flight, the airline made an exception and let them work together this one time. It was horrible to hear stories on TV about the flight attendants possibly being tortured and killed first. A few months later the only remains they could find were returned to my Aunt Britt and Uncle Bob, Jennifer's parents: her charred flight bag.

After everything I'd been through, I had developed a "just keep going" attitude and continued with the tour. Suddenly the new look I had been sporting with no lasting side effects became a big issue at every airport I entered. Before September 11, sometimes the airport security men would lean over and say something like, "Great beard, man. Wish I could grow one like that." But now I was a security threat and was always singled out of the line for interrogation. It got so bad that I had to shave.

Once I got back to America and rested a little, I started to develop a fear of flying, like many people probably did after the attacks. The flight back from Europe to Los Angeles was terrifying. I kept imagining that we were about to fly into a building at any moment. I didn't want to end up like those body parts I saw on the street when the plane crashed in my neighborhood. I had the upcoming U.S. tour routed so I wouldn't ever have to fly. I rode on the bus all the way from Los Angeles to the first stop in Austin, Texas. The rest of the band flew.

Wim Wenders, the director of the films *Paris, Texas* and *Wings of Desire,* had written a film he wanted me to act in. I thought about it and, although the idea terrified me, I decided that I should rise to the challenge. I had become friends with the actress Jennifer Jason Leigh while contributing music for her film *The Anniversary Party,* and she offered to give me free acting lessons if I came to New York. I couldn't pass up the chance to be trained by one of the best actresses in the world. But I was still scared to fly, so I decided to take the train across the country. It took four days each way, but I enjoyed having nothing to do but read, listen to music, and work on album concept ideas. Ultimately, I decided not to be in the film, but Jennifer's training was a great experience that I felt lucky to have, if I used it or not. And I got something unexpected out of the trip.

Hanging out in the dining car or the club car, I'd sit and talk with and listen to the old guys who worked on the train. I started to notice that the American passenger rail system was on its last legs. It felt like it was just barely functioning, an anachronism in the fast-changing modern world. And I noticed that I felt a certain amount of identification with this concept in terms of being a musician and songwriter in the fast-changing modern music business. I thought about Lenny Waronker, who was such a respected figure in the music business, and who was in it for the right reasons—he loved music—and how it was starting to feel like there wasn't a place for someone like that anymore. I started to hatch the idea for a song where I compared my feelings to one of these old guys with a barely certain present and certainly uncertain future working on the train. I bought a railroad almanac to look up some of the old train lines that had run through the area where I grew up in Virginia but had long since been paved over.

> *Feel like an old railroad man*
> *Ridin' out on the Bluemont line*
> *Hummin' along Old Dominion Blues*
> *Not much to see and not much left to lose*
> *And I know I can walk along the tracks*
> *It may take a little longer but I'll know*
> *How to find my way back*
>
> *I feel like an old railroad man*
> *Who's really tried the best that he can*
> *To make his life add up to something good*

But this engine no longer burns on wood
And I guess I may never understand
The times that I live in
Are not made for a railroad man

By now, things are so fucked up in the music business that in order for a truly great artist like Johnny Cash to seem relevant, he has to record cover versions of young hipster songs to appeal to young hipsters. Here's one of the greatest natural talents of his time, awkwardly singing songs that don't come naturally to him at all, something I find as indignant as Frank Sinatra singing "LA Is My Lady," his blatant and unsuitable stab at hopping on the disco bandwagon when disco was the latest thing. Johnny was just fine as an old railroad man, if you ask me.

On the train back I'm going through some of the songs for the album that I've been working on in bits and pieces for years. Most of them are pretty songs with intricate string, woodwind and brass arrangements. I listen to one I'd written years earlier called "Blinking Lights." Then I hear the same song, but without my singing on it, just instrumental. I think about how my life has had a lot of terrible moments but also so many great moments, like little lights that blink on and off on a Christmas tree. I get excited about calling the unnamed album I've been trying to put together for years *Blinking Lights* and having a version of the song that I sing, and then another version of the song for the listener to sing along with. I want the record to be pretty and compassionate. Like it's a friend to whoever is listening.

> *Blinking lights on the airplane wings*
> *Up above the trees*
> *Blinking down a morse code signal*
> *Especially for me*
> *Ain't no rainbow in the sky*
> *In the middle of the night*
> *But the signal's coming through*
> *One day I will be alright again*

I return home refreshed and eager to work on the album. But the process quickly becomes tedious. One day as I'm standing in Jim Lang's studio while we go over mapping out a string arrangement on his computer for the billionth time, I become so bored and frustrated that I start to hatch the plan for a whole new record in my mind as we're going through the motions. I'm thinking about the Muddy Waters records that I've been listening to lately and how much I admire the simple, direct, and succinct songwriting and performing on them. Suddenly I'm *dying* to get the band together from the tour a few months ago in a room, plug in some electric guitars, and play like a band wailing away in the garage. I can't take anymore of this sterile environment. As soon as I get home that night I call everyone and make a plan to make a new record as soon as possible.

The next morning I go down to the basement and start writing songs for it, two or three a day.

Meanwhile, Butch and I are having money troubles. He's been out moonlighting with other acts and isn't happy with our arrangement anymore. We agree to keep working together but on a more casual, less permanent basis. He comes in to play on the sessions for the new record before he sets out on another tour. We set up in a circle and play as a live band for ten days. The result is an album I name *Shootenanny!*. I figured the crazy times we were living in were calling out for someone to come up with a funny name for a shooting spree. Why not me?

When I turn the record in to the label, they are more excited about it than any other record I've ever made. Presidents from all departments of the label call me at home to congratulate me. Unlike the last couple of albums I'd turned in, there is a "buzz" around the offices about the new EELS album, and a release date is immediately set.

During the months between turning the album in and its release, something is going on behind the scenes at the record company that we don't know about. If the company does not make a certain amount of money that year, they will have to be sold to a larger conglomerate. So only acts with the biggest mainstream moneymaking potential matter to them now. We don't know it, but the excitement over *Shootenanny!* has now secretly become total apathy.

On my fortieth birthday I'm in London, getting carsick

on my way to do a photo shoot at a bird sanctuary in the cold, pouring rain (*I Like Birds*—get it?). I'm older than my older sister ever was, which is weird. Must keep going. I don't tell anyone it's my birthday.

Back at home, I watch Elvis's 1968 TV "comeback special" one night and decide that I have to dress the band in red polyester suits like Elvis's band. We go around the world twice, playing more than eighty shows.

One of my greatest musical heroes, Tom Waits, is a judge for the Shortlist Music Prize, which aims to be kind of an anti-Grammy awards, honoring talent instead of popularity. He nominates *Shootenanny!*, which brings a feeling of validation and a much needed dose of self-esteem that actually penetrates my skin and sticks with me a little. I've never thought any awards meant anything, but having one of your musical heroes like something you did to the point of nominating it for an award—that's pretty nice.

One morning during the tour I wake up in St. Louis to the sound of my hotel-room phone ringing. I get the news that our friend Elliott Smith has died back in Echo Park.

The first time I met Elliott, back in 1996, I walked out of the room and pulled one of our mutual friends aside and said, "I'm worried about this guy." He was a super sweet and quiet guy who didn't appear to have any armor to protect himself, and he was on the rise in the music business—not a good place for the armorless, it turns out.

I felt really strong and safe in comparison, and that's saying something.

I remembered one of the last times I saw him, we were sitting on the couch in the office at Largo, the Los Angeles club where Elliott and I both played at often. Lisa Germano was telling Elliott and me a story about something that had recently happened to her. Flanagan, the owner of Largo, had a big, white, fluffy dog named Seamus, who had just jumped up on the couch and squeezed in behind Lisa. As she continues her story, Seamus throws his front paws over Lisa's shoulders and starts humping her back, but Lisa appears to be oblivious and continues her story. Flanagan and I are laughing so hard we're crying, but Elliott just kept leaning forward and listening to Lisa's story, trying to give her the dignity to finish, even though a big white dog was straddling her and furiously pumping away on her back.

That same night I got up on the stage to play a few songs. I finished with George Bush's favorite, "It's a Motherfucker," and walked off stage into the dark. As the house music started up I felt a hand on my shoulder. I turned to see Elliott standing there in the dark. "Nice song," he said. If anyone knew that it is, indeed, a motherfucker, it was Elliott.

He found a way to give himself some armor and in later years his personality took on a massive change as a result of the kinds of drugs he was taking. I started to hear stories about him buying disposable camera after disposable camera so he could snap photos of a car that he was convinced was constantly following him. One night Elliott gave me his new number and said he'd like to get together to play guitars and see what happens, which I really wanted to do. But I waited too long to call. Once he got into this dark period, I was too scared to go through with it. I think Elliott and my sister, Liz, had a lot in common at this point and I'd already had enough of it, I'm sorry to say.

———

IN MANCHESTER, ENGLAND, I GET SICK AND lose my voice just before the show is to begin. It's sold out and the audience is already in. We're told that if we cancel the show the rowdy Manchester crowd is likely to riot. A doctor comes to give me a shot, and I spend an hour with my head under a towel breathing steam. It works enough to get me through the show, but the rigors of touring are taking their toll and I keep getting bad colds from sweating on stage and freezing on the bus or catching people's shit on all the planes I have to be on. (I eventually got over my fear of flying just in time to develop a fear of catching people's germs while flying.) My voice sounds bad most of the year and loses much of its range and power. When I get home, I have to have surgery to remove a large cyst that has developed in my sinus. A week after the operation, I go to the doctor to get the packs removed from my nose. As they pull them out, I feel the most exquisite physical pain I have ever felt, as if my brain is being pulled out through my nose.

In Montreal, Lenny calls me in my hotel room to tell me that DreamWorks Records is being sold to Universal Music and that he and Mo will not be part of it anymore. I'm incredibly sad to be losing Lenny and Mo, but I also notice a strange excitement at the uncertainty of my future. I've come to appreciate the curveballs that keep getting thrown at me and I'm going to try to trust this one. I go out to a pool hall in Montreal to drink beer and play pool with the band.

15

BLINKING LIGHTS (FOR ME)

I'M STANDING ON THE STAINED, FADED BABY blue carpet in Johnny Cash's bedroom. The room is empty except for Johnny and June's bed, a portrait of them on the wall, and the lift that was installed to get Johnny up and down the first and second floors of his home during his final years. June died and Johnny sweetly followed her soon after. (I predicted he would go within three months after she died; he made it four.) I'm at his house outside of Nashville looking at buying some of his land. I stand alone in the hidden library behind the bedroom where Johnny would sit for hours with his guitar and books, imagining him sitting there, looking up from a book to smile at me. I walk over to June's ornate bathroom to take a piss. It's all so sad, I think to myself. That amazing life, and here's what's left. An empty house with a stained carpet. It's reminding me too much of being in my family's house after they had all died. I decide not to buy the land. Not long after, Johnny and June's home burns to the ground.

———

ONE OF MY FAVORITE PASTIMES IS WONDERING how much time could pass between the moment I die and when my body is found. I spend so much time alone that I am probably a prime candidate to be one of those people who dies and isn't discovered for days or weeks. Would my hound dog, Bobby, Jr., be forced to eat my carcass because I wasn't alive to feed him?

I have to think about stuff like this, I guess, because, at this point, it sure seems like I'm around death a lot. I can always feel it knocking at the door. I recently went on vacation with the band, my first vacation in ten years, and I noticed something interesting. Everyone wanted to go down to the beach during the day, and stare at the stars in the sky at night. I noticed that I seemed more bored with these activities than the others. I realized that people probably liked to look at the vast horizon of the beach and the endless sky at night because it took them out of their daily routine and reminded them about bigger things. But I never seem to stop thinking about these bigger things.

While recovering from the surgery after the tour, I spent the winter resting and, for once, not working on anything. I just sat around thinking a lot and passing the hours entertaining myself any way I could. Answering wrong-number phone calls for the local video store, whose number is one digit away from mine, became a time-consuming hobby. A kid asks if we have the latest action/adventure film, I put him on hold while he thinks I'm checking the shelves for it, then get back on and tell him we're out of it. Then I ask him if he's read the book. He says no and I ask him when was the last time he read *any* book? He says it's been a while and I tell him he should go to the library and read something. He says OK. I get a lot of these calls and impersonating a video-store clerk becomes one of my chief means of passing the hours.

It got to the point where I was getting tired of thinking so much and doing nothing but talking to kids who think I'm a video-store clerk. An idea started to form in my mind. I should try to make an album that, like the Kubrick and Bergman films that I loved, was more important to feel than to think about. At this point I had been working on the idea of the *Blinking Lights* album having a linear story line, from birth to death and all ages in between. But now that felt too specific and too much like a rock opera or something. I decided it shouldn't be so specific and it should also have instrumental passages and plenty of breathing room spread over two discs. I wanted it to be full of life and love. I wanted it to be about the idea of God, and the God that's in the details, whatever God is. I wanted it to be about the condition of living. I got excited about working again.

Yes, I'd been through some terrible stuff. But I couldn't ignore the fact that I'd been through a lot of great stuff, too, and I wanted to reflect that in my songs. One morning, while I was brushing my teeth, I looked in the bathroom mirror. My father was looking back at me. I realized I could identify with him in a lot of ways now. I was learning more from reading about him. How he was depressed from feeling underappreciated or misunderstood, how he wanted to be left alone. How he wore the same clothes all the time, just like me. I realized that I had been feeling that same thing he must have been feeling all those years when he couldn't be bothered because he always had some crazy ideas he was trying to sort out in his head. You're just about to crack the code and the kid wants to play baseball. I get it now. We're both "idea men" and anything outside of these ideas is a distraction. I had been angry at him all these years, but now that I saw so much of him in myself, it became easy to identify with him. I let him off the hook. And life immediately got better. My parents didn't have a clue how to raise children, it's true. But I can see that, given what they were given, they gave it their best shot.

And being through the hardships in my life made the other times in my life something I could really dig into and appreciate. Anything is fun compared to cleaning your emaciated mother's shit off of her, right?

I wanted to celebrate life. That meant all the ups and downs. I realized how lucky I was to have had some of the seemingly horrible experiences I did because it meant I was one of the lucky people who experiences a wide spectrum of some of life's situations.

A colleague of my father's once said that, just a day or two before he died, my father had told him that he felt he had lived a good life and that if he were to die right then, he was satisfied. I guess since he died a couple of days later, we should all be careful about making such pronouncements, but I thought about it and I could kind of see why he felt that way. The tougher circumstances I'd been through were now making it easier for me to truly appreciate all the great things in my life. I lived in a house that I loved being in, had some good friends, and was able to actually make a living doing what I love and have to do. How often do people really get to be in that position?

I was still having occasional bouts of desperation and hopelessness, but I felt stronger, like it wasn't going to overtake me. I wanted to express how grateful I was for the terrible experiences as well as the great experiences of my life. I thought about the moment when I heard that Liz had died and my legs gave out as I fell on the floor.

Do you know what it's like to fall on the floor
Cry your guts out 'til you got no more
Hey man now you're really living
Have you ever made love to a beautiful girl
Made you feel like it's not such a bad world
Hey man now you're really living

Now you're really giving everything
And you're really getting all you gave
Now you're really living what
This life is all about

Well I just saw the sun rise over the hill
Never used to give me much of a thrill
But hey man now I'm really living

Do you know what it's like to care too much
'Bout someone that you're never gonna get to touch
Hey man now you're really living
Have you ever sat down in the fresh cut grass
And thought about the moment and when it will
    pass
Hey man now you're really living

It seems like whenever I'm not working on new music I start to wither and die. I feel rejuvenated after not knowing what to do with myself for a while. I'm the happiest I can ever remember being while I'm recording these new songs in the basement. I work for several months, two weeks of recording then two weeks off just to listen, sequence, edit, and figure out what to throw out and what is needed for the next two weeks of recording. Back and forth like this for months.

One day I find myself on the phone with my hero Tom Waits speaking on the other end. I can't believe that I'm talking to Tom Waits, the artist I've admired for so long and couldn't imagine as a real person offstage—but there's no mistaking that the gravelly voice on the other end of the line belongs to him. Later, the person who gave my number to Tom asks me if it was OK to give my number out. I tell her that I don't like my number to be passed around, but if John Lennon, Bob Dylan, or Tom Waits ask for it, it's OK to give it out.

As I'm talking to Tom, I summon up the courage to ask him if he'd be interested in doing something on the album I'm working on. He says he would, but it would have to be on a four-track cassette tape so he can record his contribution the way he likes to, in his bathroom. I immediately get off the phone and get my old four-track cassette recorder out of the closet, only to learn that it records at twice the speed of Tom's four-track recorder. I bring this up to my recording engineer, Ryan, and we realize that the best thing to do is to look on eBay for the same model Tom owns, and we find one immediately, which is sent over the next day. I record my parts onto two tracks of the cassette tape and leave the other two tracks for Tom to fill. I send the tape to him with detailed instructions of what I want him to do. He ignores my instructions completely, accidentally erases my lead vocal track, and sends me back a tape of him stomping on his bathroom floor, yelling and crying like a baby. You don't tell Tom Waits what to do. It's great. He's very apologetic for erasing my vocal and offers to do yard work at my house to make up for it. I, of course, am thrilled by the whole thing. *Tom Waits erased my vocal.*

I meet with an A&R guy that I've been shuffled to at Interscope, the Universal company that is now in charge of DreamWorks Records' rotting carcass. I tell him about this sprawling double album that has become a mission to me that I must complete. He says things about what a respected artist I am and how his label is the right place for me and this project. I feel good after the meeting.

After many months, one day I listen to the latest version of the album and notice that I don't have any nagging feelings left about what needs to change. I know I'm done. I tell the managers I'm going to start the mastering process, where final EQ (sound equalization) is added as my recordings are turned into a master to be manufactured. The managers call the A&R guy and tell him the label can hear some of the album now. The A&R guy says, "I don't think this is the right place for him," and doesn't even ask to hear any of the record.

The triumphant feeling of having finished recording the album vanishes as I now realize that I've just made (and paid for) a gigantic thirty-three-track double album that the record company doesn't even want to listen to, let alone put out. Not knowing what else to do, I continue with the mastering process, which normally takes a day or two for most artists but goes on to take three months to complete in this case. The first place I take it to doesn't have a clue what to do with it and shuffles me to the back of the line. Then I take it to my friend Dan Hersch, who has mastered some of our live albums. The album is very dynamic and complicated in some ways. There are very quiet, pretty parts and then loud crashing parts. It's very difficult to get it right from song to song, so it flows and has the proper impact that I want it to have as a whole. I've become obsessed with the album at this point, and I feel psychologically and physically unable to let go of it until it is exactly how I want and know it should be.

Ray Charles dies and they set his body out in a coffin at the Los Angeles Convention Center for a public viewing. I am one of the first people in line to see Brother Ray's last show. When I get home that afternoon, Dan Hersch calls me and asks if I have a gun. He's been making intricate mastering changes at my request for months and has reached a point where he'd rather blow his head off than work on this album anymore. I hang up the phone and lie down. I also feel like I want to blow my head off. I feel totally alone and wonder how I got into this situation where I've spent all my energy and money making a huge behemoth of an album that no one asked for. I've been working on the songs for seven years and now it feels like no one cares either way. I feel like I'm the only one who cares about it, and I've put everything I have into it. Ironically, making this album about embracing and celebrating life has made me miserable and suicidal.

16

THINGS THE GRANDCHILDREN SHOULD KNOW

"HOW IS IT POSSIBLE?"

I'm sitting in a posh hotel in Paris. Mick Jagger is having tea in the lobby. I'm stuck in the drafty conference room doing a TV interview. The French TV journalist is asking me about the song "Things the Grandchildren Should Know," that's about to come out on the *Blinking Lights and Other Revelations* double album, which is finally being released, a year after I finished it.

"Do you have children?" the TV journalist asks in her heavily accented English.

I sit back in the wooden chair they've offered me.

"Not yet. I'm gonna go straight to grandchildren," I say.

She blinks and stares blankly back at me, squinting and squeezing her eyebrows down.

"But . . . how is it possible?"

"Uh, well . . . think about it; it's a much better deal," I say, shifting in my chair. "With grandchildren, you just see them on the weekend. Then you get the rest of the week to yourself."

"But how is it possible?"

"I don't know. I'll figure it out."

"But . . . it is not possible . . ."

I've found myself in a situation that I often find myself in, where my sense of humor doesn't translate well in a foreign country. It's an endearing trait, how they take everything literally. I like that about them, but I have to keep reminding myself not to be funny at foreign interviews. But the only way I can get through most of them is to do things like this to entertain myself.

I usually dislike doing interviews but I'm happy to be spreading the word about the *Blinking Lights* album since it was such a long, hard road getting it out, even harder than the other hard-to-get-out records I'd made. After feeling like it was unwanted for so long and after working so hard and being virtually consumed by the mission, it felt good that people cared about it now.

After DreamWorks was sold to Universal and the Interscope A&R guy who seemed so gung-ho about my "artistry" then told my manager that it wasn't the right place for me after all, I was paid out of my contract and allowed to take the *Blinking Lights* album with me. Money for nothing, as they say. They didn't even ask to hear a single note of the album. Then I signed on with Vagrant Records, which was owned by Interscope and Universal anyway, so it's one of those great stories where the artist sort of gets paid twice by the same company. Now I had a *third* chance. This cat has seen some tough times, but he's already living his third life, you know?

After endless months of sitting around the house depressed, my spirits are lifted when a release date is finally set for the album and rave reviews start pouring in. It's getting four and five star reviews all over. The kind of thing I'd taken for granted in the past means more to me now after the lonely feeling of being the only one who cared about the album for so long. The *Souljacker* debacle was merely a warm-up act for this one. That experience had been vindicating but the *Blinking Lights* situation could not have been lonelier, so this was really hitting home.

Reviews don't really mean anything if you look at the history of rock journalism. They usually can't tell what will stand the test of time when they review something brand new on a tight deadline, but I'm going to let myself feel good about this. (Book reviewers: this doesn't mean you, of course. I have nothing but the utmost respect for what you do. How do you like the book so far?) Tom Waits calls to tell me the album reminds him of a baked Alaska. I think about it and quickly deduce that comparing my album to flaming ice cream can only be the greatest of compliments coming from Tom Waits. It all feels good. Once again, I feel vindicated for sticking to my guns. In this case, it feels even better than the other times, because I'd really gone out on a limb, spending my own money to make this mammoth double album that no one had asked for or seemingly wanted. And it was such a long, lonely battle to get it out. It turned out that the Vagrant people were a lot better suited to getting my record out to people who would like it. Record companies hate double albums, but they accepted it and liked it just as it was. Even though it was a double album and was getting no significant radio airplay, it charted higher than any of my other records had, even *Beautiful Freak*: the one that was all over MTV and all that. But this one wasn't getting any of that kind of exposure. It was just being appreciated on its own merits. We played all the big TV shows: *Jay Leno*, *David Letterman*, etc., but rather than play the same "single" on every show, as acts normally do, we played a different song from the album on each TV show.

During the endless months between finishing the album and it finally being released, I had taken up the practice of spending evenings sitting out on the front porch of my guesthouse in the backyard, smoking cigars and playing old records on the record player. After the rigors and sickness of the last tour, and the subsequent surgery I had to endure as a result, I had decided that I was done with touring. The physical toll it took on me was just too much. But as I was sitting there in front of the guesthouse one night, looking at the cigar smoke I was blowing out of my mouth as it floated up into the night sky, I started to imagine a concert where I was smoking a cigar on stage. I thought about how fun and challenging it would be to put together a show that was so different from the other shows I'd done. I could see a string quartet sitting where the drum set usually was and lots of antique instruments. We'd all dress up in nice evening attire and I'd have a cigar and the cane I used when I'd hurt my leg a few years ago. A gentlemen's EELS concert. I got so excited about it that I immediately knew I had to do it and couldn't stop myself from running inside to start making calls to put it all together.

It was difficult getting all the string arrangements and logistics together, but really satisfying to set some of the old songs in such a drastically new light. The "EELS with strings" tour went around the world twice, and although I was told it was too elaborate a show for its own good—i.e., it was going to lose tons of money—it turned out to be a big success. After all these years, it seemed like I was being rewarded for not giving in.

That's not to say that there weren't the usual awkward moments here and there. It seems like I often get punished for being a year ahead or behind people's expectations. One year someone will come to one of the shows and love the acoustic guitar and pretty melodies that they hear. Then they feel betrayed when they come another year and hear the sound of a hundred buses crashing into each other coming out of my stack of guitar amps. The opposite can happen as well. One person loves the bus crash sound and then feels betrayed if the next time isn't so loud and rollicking. One year we play with saxophones and acoustic guitars—between a hardcore German rap act and Nine Inch Nails. The next year we bring electric guitars and blaring, buzzy synthesizers—and play between David Byrne doing spoken word and an author reading from his latest book. We're always getting booked to play places based on what they saw us do the year before, and it gets us into a lot of inappropriate situations when we show up doing something completely different from what they saw last time.

During the "with strings" tour one night in Germany, a concertgoer calls out *"YOU ARE BORING!"* between songs. He's German and he wants to rock. We play him a Scorpions riff, but it isn't enough. Again, I just don't understand why some people want everything to sound like what they expect. Life's too short for such boring predictability. *You* are boring, sir.

When we play on a TV show in England, we are set up in a circle with four other acts in a huge television studio, each playing a song before the next band plays. Van Morrison is set up right next to us. Fifty feet across from us in the huge airplane-hangar-like studio is the new faux soul singer, John Legend. After our first song, a production assistant makes the long walk over from John Legend's side of the studio and whispers in my ear, "Mr. Legend wants you to put your cigar out."

Mr. Legend? I'm fifty feet away from him and none of the smoke could ever reach him or pose any kind of a problem or threat to his health in this gigantic, high-ceilinged room. You see this kind of divalike behavior a lot with new acts who aren't sure how to rein in the new feelings of power that success has brought. I put the cigar out between songs for Mr. Legend (real name, John Stephens) but, as it is a theatrical device integral to our performance, I have to light it up briefly when our next song comes along. At the end of the show, as the host introduces and thanks us, the sound of Mr. Legend loudly booing is heard on TV sets tuned to the BBC all over England. To contrast Mr. Legend's pomposity, Van Morrison, an *actual* legend, cordially asks me if my cigar is Cuban. A real legend doesn't have to name himself one. Or act like a twat.

———

DURING THE COURSE OF THE LONG TOUR, WE
play at some of my favorite, legendary halls around the

world. Town Hall in New York, where so many great live records have been made; Royal Festival Hall in London; Patti Smith invites us to be part of a festival she is curating at Queen Elizabeth Hall in London. Toward the end of the long tour, we come back for one more show in London, at the Royal Albert Hall. Besides the fact that it's such a legendary, beautifully ornate old concert hall, and our biggest London show to date, I'm excited about it because of the history the stage itself has held: The Beatles and The Rolling Stones (on the same night, no less), The Who, Bob Dylan, Jimi Hendrix, Led Zeppelin . . . and, of course, John Lennon sang about it in "A Day in the Life," a record I played over and over on the living-room record player when I was a little kid back in Virginia.

I'm extremely nervous all day as we sound check and prepare for the Albert Hall show. As I stand on the stage, I worry if I'm worthy to be standing in the same place as so many of my heroes (even though I've written a book about my kooky life, I don't think that I am). But as the hall fills with people, the lights go down, and I step out onto the stage, I feel an unusual sense of calm. I don't feel nervous at all tonight, which is odd because I usually feel nervous *every* night, and this is a big night. But something has clicked in me and I'm fine all of the sudden. I play songs from all different parts of my life, and I feel acutely tuned into the feelings I had when I wrote each song as I'm singing them.

Ten pounds and a head of hair
Came into without a care
What they thought were cries were little laughs
Only looking forward and moving fast

As I sing, I think about the baby pictures of me I found in my mom's attic. Although I grew into being a scrawny ectomorph, I was, indeed, quite a fat baby, weighing in at nearly ten pounds. I think about my poor mother, when she had me that night in the Washington, D.C., hospital. That must've hurt.

How does her world spin
Without me in her nest
Could there really be such happiness?

As the words come out of my mouth, I'm not noticing the three thousand people staring back at me. I'm thinking about the irrational crush I had on the girl at the post office back in Virginia. I'm glad she's not here to hear me utter the embarrassing words I wrote about her.

My beloved monster and me
If she wants she will disrobe you
But if you lay her down for a kiss
Her little heart, it might explode

I think about the half-hour Jon Brion allotted me to write in my basement that night in Echo Park and how many thousands of times and ways I've played this song since.

The show is going great. It's a special night with some indefinable feeling of magic hanging in the air. Finally, it's time to end the show, and I strum the opening guitar chord of the song that had confounded the French TV journalist months earlier. I start to sing in a relaxed, conversational tone:

> *I go to bed real early*
> *Everybody thinks it's strange*
> *I get up early in the morning*
> *No matter how disappointed I was*
> *With the day before*
> *It feels new*

Just living another day has always felt like some sort of a success to me. I hear my voice echoing off the cavernous Albert Hall walls and bouncing back at me. I look out at all the people there, who seem genuinely interested in what I have to say. I think about the night I sat in my backyard smoking a cigar, dreaming up the show I was performing at this very moment. How I sat there looking up into the cigar smoke floating into the sky and dreamed up an elaborate scene that I was now living in. How amazing, to be able to do that, I think.

I don't leave the house much
I don't like being around people
Makes me nervous and weird
I don't like going to shows either
It's better for me to stay home
Some might think it means I hate people
But that's not quite right

I do some stupid things
But my heart's in the right place
And this I know

I feel like I did the day I wrote this song, when I went down to the basement, plugged in an electric guitar, and sat down to write a song about how all the hard times must've been worth it because I was genuinely happy that day. I felt a new sense of self-acceptance. Sure, I'm a weirdo in some ways. I don't like going to parties and shows, I hide in my house a lot. But, all things considered, it could be a lot worse. And I'm able to get myself to *this* show, at least. I become aware of a feeling that has been slowly creeping in under my skin for years, but has now become more tangible. I'd been through a lot but—*I'm OK*. And if I want to be, I'm better than OK. I'm certainly not the most well-adjusted person on Earth, but considering everything . . . I mean—I *survived*. And I survived just by being me. How lucky and amazing is that?

I got a dog
I take him for a walk
And all the people like to say hello
I'm used to staring down at the sidewalk cracks
I'm learning how to say hello
Without too much trouble

I feel a warmth and sense of community as I look out at the sea of orange faces in the audience glowing from the stage lights. We're all fucked up, I'm thinking, and that's the truth. Everyone's got some crazy shit going on in their life and no one is living any of that fairy-tale shit that the TV made you believe life was supposed to be like when you were young.

I'm turning out just like my father
Though I swore I never would
Now I can say that I have love for him
I never really understood
What it must have been like for him
Living inside his head
I feel like he's here with me now
Even though he's dead

I feel exhilarated now that I've forgiven my dad for any shortcomings he had as a father. Like a weight is lifted off my shoulders. I understand why you hear people talk about how holding a grudge does more harm to yourself than the person the grudge is against when I can actually feel a physical lightness to my being as I sing these words. I think about how angry I was that my dad didn't take better care of himself. How he never went to the doctor, let himself become grossly overweight, smoked three packs a day, drank like a fish, and never exercised. But then I think about how his colleague mentioned that, days before dying, my dad had said that he had lived a good life and that he was satisfied. I realize that there is a certain value in my father's way of life. He ate, smoked, and drank as he pleased, and one day he just suddenly and quickly died. Given some of the other choices I'd witnessed, it turns out that enjoying yourself and then dying quickly is not such a bad way to go.

> *It's not all good and it's not all bad*
> *Don't believe everything you read*
> *I'm the only one who knows what it's like*
> *So I thought I'd better tell you*
> *Before I leave*

I think about how my father never said much to me, and how I wish he had just sat down and shot straight with me. What if I have a kid someday who wants to know what it was like inside *my* head? The French TV journalist was right. I don't even have kids yet, let alone grandchildren.

There's still time. I better write down what it's been like to be me so they won't have to wonder the way I do about my father.

I remember a photo I found when I was cleaning out the attic in Virginia after my mom died. It was a photo of my great-grandfather standing above my grandfather, who was standing above my father, who is holding my sister Liz when she was a baby. Hugh I, Hugh Jr., Hugh III, and Liz. *Four generations* of Everetts all in the same room, standing like some flesh, family totem pole. Now there was only me, and all the pressure that feeling of heritage brings with it. If the family name is to continue, it's all on my shoulders now. I don't know if I can handle it. How could there have been four living generations so recently and now there is only me?

> *So in the end I'd like to say*
> *That I'm a very thankful man*
> *I tried to make the most of my situations*
> *And enjoy what I had*
> *I knew true love and I knew passion*
> *And the difference between the two*
> *And I had some regrets*
> *But if I had to do it all again*
> *Well, it's something I'd like to do*

All the hard times, I'm thinking, all the crazy shit. All

the amazing times. Images are racing through my head. Looking at my first-grade classmates through tears after being accused of cheating. Lying in my bunk bed, kissing my first girlfriend. Running barefoot past plane seats, windows, and ashtrays on my street. Robert coming at me with a butcher knife. Lifting my father's body off the bed. My mom laughing while I dole out her medicine. Closing Liz's casket.

I look out at the Albert Hall audience. I think about how I wanted to drive off that bridge when I was a teenager and how I'd been told that I would starve if I tried to do something with my music. If only someone could've told me when I was younger that one day I'd be standing on the stage at the Royal Albert Hall, singing my songs to thousands of appreciative listeners. I hear the string quartet swell behind me and feel a shiver shoot up my spine that moves out to my fingertips and scalp.

That feeling I had when I was a teenager—that I wouldn't live to see eighteen—I don't have that kind of feeling anymore. I think I used thoughts like that as some kind of safety valve. To feel like there was some way out. But now I have no inkling what lies ahead. I like getting older. It's taken me this long to start to feel a little comfortable being me. Sure was a long way around to getting there, but it's what I had to do. Was either that or die, so it feels like a triumph.

As I strum the final chord of the song, my guitar strap

breaks and I catch the bottom of the guitar and hold it against my torso, reminding me that life never runs totally smooth and nothing ever goes according to plan. I think to myself, It figures, as I walk off the stage. The crowd stands up and applauds enthusiastically, shouting out for another encore. I'm thinking about how I never had a plan, so it didn't really matter if life didn't go according to one. But I had to admit that, for someone who had no plan, all things considered, things had turned out pretty well at this moment.

I may or may not outrun the family demons, I don't know. But I have to say that I'm proud that I've made it this far, and if this is as far as it goes—not bad, sir. Some extreme downs, but certainly some extreme ups, don't you think? I think again about what my dad said a few days before he died, that he had had a good life, and I now realized that I felt the same way. What a life it's already been. To be able to survive the hard stuff and enjoy the soft stuff. Hey, man, indeed. Now I really am living.

NOW WHAT?

I WAKE UP IN THE BACK OF A BUS, DESPERATELY needing to poop. I've had three hours of sleep and you can't go "number two" on a tour bus. The toilet can only handle "number one." I scan the bus floor for some pants and change out of my pajamas. I slip my jeans on (one leg at a time, just like you, gentle reader) and stagger up towards the front of the bus, tripping on someone's balled-up socks in the corridor. Everyone else is asleep in their bunks. It's dark and smelly as I pass through the "Hall of Snores." The sound of twelve people wheezing in unison behind their bunk curtains is like a symphony of locusts being run over by lawn mowers. It's too much for my sleep-deprived, aching head. It smells like ass in here. Must get out. This would be a lot more fun if I was nineteen. I finally get to the front and write a note to the bus driver, so he won't drive to the next city without me. I put the note on the driver's seat so he won't miss it:

LOOKING FOR A PLACE TO POOP.
BACK SOON. DON'T LEAVE WITHOUT ME.
–E

I open the bus door and step off. The morning sun blares straight through my Ray-Bans into my bloodshot eyes. It's early Saturday morning and I'm standing in front of the Roxy Theatre on the Sunset Strip where we've just played some extremely loud tour warm-up shows the previous two nights. My ears are still ringing. I start shuffling my way down Sunset Boulevard, looking for a restaurant where I can buy some token item in order to use their bathroom. I'm so tired that just lifting my feet off the pavement to walk is difficult.

As I'm walking down the sidewalk, I look down and notice that I'm wearing my plaid old-man slippers. I forgot to put my shoes on. I start to feel stupid and conspicuous, but I'm too tired and desperate for a bathroom to really care. I finally come upon Duke's coffee shop, walk in and buy an iced tea at the counter. I walk to the back of the room where I see a sign that says MEN above a door. I enter the bathroom and find an insane homeless man using the only toilet, muttering gibberish, grunting and repeatedly flushing the toilet. I desperately have to go to the bathroom but I have to wait for the insane guy to finish his grunting and flushing. None of this is unusual. This is how most of my mornings start these days.

A few weeks later, our European double-decker bus goes under a bridge somewhere in Europe that is a few inches lower than the top of our bus. Amazingly, no one is hurt, but I spend much of the rainy season setting up pots and pans to catch water coming through our patched-together roof before it hits my bunk. Soon after, at 3 a.m. one early morning in Alabama, a truck driver falls asleep at the wheel, forcing our bus off the highway just as we're entering a bridge. We go up on the concrete embankment and blow out most of the right-side tires. I wake up flying off my bunk, thinking I'm about to die. Amazingly again, no one is seriously hurt. We spend the day on the side of the road in Alabama waiting for a succession of the wrong tires to be put on, yet somehow make it to New Orleans that night just in time to rock the fuck out of a city that sorely needs rocking the fuck out of.

I start to have crazy dreams on the bus. Like this one: I'm riding shotgun with my guitarist Chet, who is driving Old Gold, my old Chevy Nova. He's driving really fast and crazy through a snowy mountain road, flying off the road over bumps, soaring down, landing hard. He's laughing and I'm getting worried. He loses control of the car and we crash into a snowbank. We both crawl out of the wreckage unscathed and start walking down the mountain. When we finally get to the bottom, we're in sunny Burbank, California, at the gates of the Warner Brothers studio lot. It's a beautiful day and there are three three-legged deers grazing on grass at the studio entrance. I wave goodbye to Chet and ask the three deers if they'd like to come to work with me. I flash my studio badge to the security guard, who presses a button that lifts the gate so I can enter the studio lot. The three deers follow me and we walk to Stage 12, where I have a job as an assistant. I invite the deers to come in. As I'm changing into my uniform at my locker, my boss walks in and starts yelling at me, "Who brought these fucking three-legged deers in here?"

"I did, sir. They're with me," I say.

"Well, get them the hell out of here. You're fired!" he shouts back.

I change back into my street clothes and motion for the deers to follow me. We walk off the studio lot and down to a little neighborhood on the banks of a river nearby. We come to a nice ranch house with shady trees surrounding it. I open the front door and my wife and kids come running up to greet me.

"Daddy's home! Yay!" they all squeal in unison.

"Hey, kids! I want you to meet our new pets!" I announce, and the deers trot into the house as the kids jump up and down excitedly. Then I wake up.

The dream doesn't seem that far off from my waking life. All these crazy things are happening, but I just keep going from scene to scene, whatever comes my way. I'm like a cockroach. I just keep going. I think the constant motion of my life on tour may be making me want some stability. But this is my life. It's not ideal for a guy who prefers to hide out in his house, but it has its moments.

I still have occasional bouts of desperation where I feel like there's no hope. And I hate going to a new doctor or dentist. Not for the usual reasons, though. It's the part where you fill out the personal information form, when I get to,

IN CASE OF EMERGENCY, CONTACT:

I don't know who to put there, and it makes me really sad and embarrassed. It's the loneliest feeling, having no family. Holidays really suck and I usually try to pretend they're not happening. On the bright side, Christmas shopping is a cinch. The family I grew up with disappeared too quickly, and I've spent too many years hiding out like a lone wolf. I know that if I were to die tomorrow, my obituary could say:

Ironically, Everett, who had no children at the time of his death, let alone grandchildren, titled his autobiography Things The Grandchildren Should Know.

But circumstances have brought me here and I'm a lot wiser now, and life is full of so many surprises. This could all change at any moment. It only takes a second for your life to change in huge ways.

And if I'm such a nonbeliever, why do I keep catching myself sitting on the back porch with my head tilted toward the night sky, talking to Liz and my mom and dad?

I can get overwhelmed with situations sometimes, but it's not as bad or as often as it used to be, and I think living through so much crazy shit really has made me stronger. Just like they say it should.

People in my immediate family don't seem to live very long. But I'm still around, so maybe I'll be an exception. Maybe not. Maybe I'll live to be a hundred. Maybe I'll have grandchildren. Maybe I'll get to write volume two of this book. You never know. I don't have any idea what happens next. Neither do you.

ACKNOWLEDGMENTS

Thank you to the following people who helped with this book and its eventual realization:

Anthony Cain, Sean Coleman, Pete Townshend, Antonia Hodgson, Matthew Guma, Kevin Gasser, Rob Kirkpatrick, Adrian Tomine, Autumn deWilde, Jim Runge, and Ray Charles.

ABOUT THE AUTHOR

Mark Oliver Everett is an ordained minister and alternative rock star. He lives with his dog, Bobby, Jr., in Los Feliz, California.